PERGAMON INTERNATIONAL LIBRARY
of Science, Technology, Engineering and Social Studies
The 1000-volume original paperback library in aid of education, industrial training and the enjoyment of leisure
Publisher: Robert Maxwell, M.C.

Prospects for Peace

Other Titles of Interest

CANNIZZO, C.
The Gun Merchants

DE VOLPI, A.
Proliferation, Plutonium and Policy

FELD, B.
A Voice Crying in the Wilderness

JAPAN NATIONAL PREPARATORY COMMITTEE
A Call from Hibakusha of Hiroshima and Nagasaki

JOLLY, R.
Disarmament and World Development

KING, A.
The State of the Planet

LASZLO, E. & KEYS, D.
Disarmament—The Human Factor

NOEL-BAKER, P.
The First World Disarmament Conference and Why It Failed, 1932-1933

TAYLOR, R. & PRITCHARD, C.
The Protest Makers

A Related Journal

WORLD DEVELOPMENT

The Monthly Multidisciplinary Journal devoted to the Study
and Promotion of World Development

Editor-in-Chief: Paul P. Streeten

Encourages the publication of articles which assist in the definition of problems of development and present innovative ideas for their solution.

Free specimen copy available on request.

Prospects for Peace

by

FRANK BARNABY

PERGAMON PRESS

OXFORD · NEW YORK · TORONTO · SYDNEY · PARIS · FRANKFURT

U.K.	Pergamon Press Ltd., Headington Hill Hall, Oxford OX3 0BW, England
U.S.A.	Pergamon Press Inc., Maxwell House, Fairview Park, Elmsford, New York 10523, U.S.A.
CANADA	Pergamon of Canada, Suite 104, 150 Consumers Road, Willowdale, Ontario M2J 1P9, Canada
AUSTRALIA	Pergamon Press (Aust.) Pty. Ltd., P.O. Box 544, Potts Point, N.S.W. 2011, Australia
FRANCE	Pergamon Press SARL, 24 rue des Ecoles, 75240 Paris, Cedex 05, France
FEDERAL REPUBLIC OF GERMANY	Pergamon Press GmbH, 6242 Kronberg-Taunus, Hammerweg 6, Federal Republic of Germany

First edition 1980

British Library Cataloguing in Publication Data

Barnaby, Frank
Prospects for peace. - (Pergamon International library).
1. Atomic warfare
I. Title
358'.93 80-41667

ISBN 0 08 027399 8 (Hardcover)
ISBN 0 08 027398 X (Flexicover)

Printed and bound in Great Britain by
William Clowes (Beccles) Limited, Beccles and London

Contents

1

Why the Probability of a Nuclear War is Increasing

In this first chapter we give the framework within which the issues of this book are presented.

The world's arsenals contain tens of thousands of nuclear weapons, probably as many as 60,000. The total explosive power of these weapons is equivalent to about one and a quarter million Hiroshima bombs, or about 4 tons of TNT for every man, woman, and child on earth. If all, or a significant portion of them, were used, the consequences would be beyond imagination.

All the major cities in the Northern Hemisphere, where most nuclear warheads are aimed, would be destroyed (on average, *each* is targeted to receive the equivalent of some 2000 Hiroshima bombs). Most of this urban population would be killed by blast and fire; the rural population would be killed by radiation from fallout. Many millions of people in the Southern Hemisphere would be killed by radiation, and the disaster would not end even there. The unpredictable (and, therefore, normally ignored) long-term effects might well include changes in the global climate, severe genetic damage, and depletion of the ozone layer that protects life on earth from excessive ultraviolet radiation. No scientist can convincingly assure us that human life would survive a nuclear world war.

Utterly catastrophic though a nuclear world war would be, its probability is steadily increasing. Symptoms of the current drift to a nuclear world war include the recent propaganda campaign to try to convince us that nuclear war may not be so bad after all, that limited nuclear wars are not only possible, but may in some circumstances even be militarily effective; that civil defence measures could reduce casualties to an "acceptable level"; that essential industry should be protected against nuclear blast; that the Warsaw Treaty Organization will soon militarily overwhelm NATO (and, no doubt, the opposite is said in the East), and so on. The current hawkish mood seems to be worldwide, or at least to extend throughout official circles in most of the Northern Hemisphere.

There are a number of reasons for the drift to war. The most obvious are related to international politics. Others are connected with advances in military technology.

The Role of International Politics

International relations for the next 20 or 30 years will be fundamentally affected by the consequences of the shortage of energy supplies.

The typical Western European country needs, so it is said, an economic growth rate of 3–4 per cent a year to maintain more or less full employment, to fund the social welfare benefits to which we have become accustomed, and to prevent an erosion in our living standards. I have heard of no politically realistic way of achieving 3 or 4 per cent economic growth over the next 10 or 20 years, even given the most optimistic predictions of energy supplies. Some people, in desperation, put their faith in nuclear power to fill the energy gap. But it would be simply impossible to build nuclear power reactors fast enough to significantly help the energy problem, at least for the rest of this century. Other people argue for massive schemes of energy conservation encouraged by new life styles. But is it realistic to expect large numbers of people to suddenly and drastically change the patterns of their lives?

The most likely outcome of the energy crisis is, therefore, that economic growth will be very low, perhaps zero or even negative. This will mean much unemployment and high inflation, probably leading to political and social turmoil in the rich countries and worsening poverty in the poor countries. (North–South tension may well become a greater threat to world security than East–West tension.) And these are the very circumstances under which countries resort to military action.

Such action may actually be demanded by populations to acquire oil and other raw materials. In fact, the competition for scarce raw materials may become the most frequent cause of future wars. And military action may also be used by politicians to divert attention from worsening domestic problems.

Of all raw materials, oil is most obviously related to security, at least in the short term. This is particularly true for the USA and its major allies. Oil accounts for about a half of the total energy consumed by the USA, Western Europe and South Korea, and for as much as about three-quarters of that consumed by Japan and Taiwan.

Persian Gulf oil supplies a significant fraction of the total energy used by these countries, ranging from about a tenth for the USA to more than a half for Japan. The bulk of Gulf oil comes from Iran, Iraq, Kuwait, Saudi Arabia, and the United Arab Emirates. These five countries, therefore, hold us in the palms of their hands. Recent and current events in Afghanistan, Mecca, and Iran show how very unstable the situation in the region is.

Oil accounts for only about a third of the total energy used by the USSR, which currently produces more oil than it consumes. But the Soviet Union will become a net importer of oil by the mid-1980s. Its oil exports to its East European allies and the West will dry up and the USSR will compete for Gulf oil. Great power rivalry in the volatile Persian Gulf region will then become even more intense.

The escalation of a regional conflict to a general nuclear war is perhaps the most likely way in which a nuclear world war would start; more likely than a direct nuclear attack by one superpower on the other, although the danger of its starting by accident or miscalculation is ever present. A conflict in, say, a Third World region like the Persian Gulf might begin as a conventional war and then escalate to a limited nuclear war, using the nuclear weapons of the local powers. This could in turn escalate to a general nuclear war involving the superpowers, especially if the superpowers supplied the conventional weapons for the original conflict. And that is why both the international arms trade, now totally out of control, and nuclear weapon proliferation are so dangerous.

We seem to be on the threshold of a new round of nuclear weapon proliferation, with Pakistan the next probable nuclear power. The widening access to nuclear weapon technology goes hand in hand with the spread of peaceful nuclear technology, itself a spin-off from military programmes. Whatever the apologists for the nuclear industry say, there is a direct link between the peaceful atom and the military atom. The more nuclear reactors there are generating electricity around the world, the greater will be the number of countries acquiring the skills and the capability to produce the fissile material to make nuclear weapons. As the number of countries with nuclear weapons increases, the probability of nuclear war will increase.

The Dangers of Uncontrolled Military Technology

International politics will greatly increase the probability of a nuclear world war, but military technology will increase it even more. The most significant technological reason is that military scientists are developing weapons which will be seen as suitable for *fighting* rather than for *deterring* a nuclear war. These new weapons include very accurate and reliable ballistic missiles with warheads that can be aimed at smaller and, therefore, many more military targets than in the past. In other words, the day is coming when one country might hope to destroy its enemy's nuclear retaliatory capability by striking first.

In this context, a first strike does not mean the ability to destroy totally the other side's strategic nuclear forces in a surprise attack. What it does mean is that the attacker *perceives* that he can destroy enough of the enemy's retaliatory forces in a surprise attack to reduce the casualties he receives in a retaliatory strike to a number he regards as "acceptable" for a given political goal. (In nuclear issues, as in almost all matters of international politics, perceptions determine events; facts do not.) The more reckless the political leadership is and the more tense superpower relations are, the greater this number of casualties is likely to be. And in his calculations the attacker is likely to make assumptions about the performance of his own and the enemy's nuclear forces which suit his arguments. Specifically, military calculations are likely to be based mainly on estimates of prompt deaths and ignore the uncertain long-term effects of a nuclear war which may well be far more lethal than the early effects. (Also the sociological and psychological consequences of a total loss of all social and technical services, even though extremely serious, are likely to be ignored. For example, how many survivors of a nuclear world war would go mad or commit suicide when they realize that they have been blasted back into the Stone Age, and a radioactive one at that?) Remember that, in times of crisis, political leaders listen to their military chiefs rather than their scientific advisers.

For many years now, official nuclear policies, at least in the United States, have been based on the assumption of mutual assured destruction. The theory was that the enemy would not attack for fear that its own cities and industries would be destroyed in retaliation. Moves away from a deterrent strategy and toward a nuclear war fighting strategy (or "counterforce", as the experts call it) are being made not because the requirements of nuclear deterrence have changed. The psychology of the enemy is, after all, the same. Policies are changing because military technology has produced more precise weapons. Once available, weapons are usually deployed, and policies then have to be modified to justify (i.e. rationalize) the deployment.

Apparently Soviet nuclear strategy always has had a stronger emphasis on counterforce than US strategy, even though Soviet missiles are less accurate and reliable than their American counterparts. As the Russians improve the quality of their missiles, their counterforce doctrine will probably become more refined. And the more the two great powers adapt to counterforce doctrines and integrate many types of nuclear weapons into their military tactics and strategies, the greater will be the probability of a nuclear war because the idea that such a war is both "fightable and winnable" will gain ground.

The path from the Hiroshima bomb to a nuclear world war brought on by the characteristics of nuclear weapons themselves may, given the enormous scientific effort put into it, be a technological inevitability. Today, nearly half a million scientists work only on military research and development, about 40 per cent of all scientists employed on research. If only physicists and engineering scientists are counted, it is well over 50 per cent. Two-fifths of world research and development expenditure, about $50,000 million, is devoted to military research and development.

An effort of this magnitude cannot fail to produce staggering results. Improvements in warhead design and missile accuracy, which have virtually reached their theoretical limits, are just two examples which indicate the incredible progress made by military technology since World War II. In the next 30 years we can expect technological revolutions in space warfare, anti-submarine warfare, electronic warfare, air defence systems, navigational systems, early warning systems, command, control and communications systems, the automated battlefield, the military use of high-energy lasers, ballistic missile defence, and a number of other fields. Many of these developments will contribute to perceptions that a nuclear war is fightable and winnable, and that a first strike is feasible and even essential, on the argument that "unless we strike now the other side will soon do so".

An excellent example is anti-submarine warfare. Now that land-based intercontinental ballistic missiles are, or soon will be, vulnerable to a first strike by missiles, nuclear deterrence depends on the invulnerability of submarine-launched ballistic missiles. Nevertheless, much research is being done on anti-submarine warfare techniques by both the USA and the USSR. This will almost certainly lead, in time, to success. Even if there is no technological breakthrough—which cannot, of course, be discounted in spite of official reassurances—steady progress in limiting the damage that can be done by enemy strategic nuclear submarines will increase perceptions not only that a surprise attack may succeed but that it is essential.

The fact that the superpowers continue working so energetically on anti-submarine warfare shows that they are unable to control military science and technology even though this activity is jeopardizing their policy of nuclear deterrence, a policy the leaderships desperately want to maintain. Military scientists, by their sheer number, form a powerful political lobby.

Moreover, in the great powers vast bureaucracies have grown up to deal with military matters. (As many civilians are paid out of military budgets as there are troops in uniform.) Academics and bureaucrats join with the military and defence industries to form an academic–bureaucratic–military–industrial complex intent on maintaining and increasing military budgets and agitating for the use of every conceivable technological advance for military purposes. This complex has so much political power as to be almost politically irresistible. In fact, the nuclear arms race is now totally out of the control of political leaders. *And this is as true in the Soviet Union as it is in the United States.* The uncontrolled nuclear arms race is without doubt the greatest single threat to our survival.

This is not to deny that great efforts have been made to control military technology and to stop the nuclear arms race between the Americans and the Russians. Since World War II many of the world's most brilliant people have been actively involved in these efforts. No other problem has received so much attention in the United Nations and other international forums. Whole libraries have been written on the subject. Yet, because of the enormous political influence of those groups that continually press for greater military efforts, nuclear and other arms races go on just as fast as human skill in the American and Soviet societies allows. We are being driven toward nuclear world war by the sheer momentum of military technology.

A Hope for the Future

I am not suggesting that some evil group is plotting our destruction. But I do suggest that we may not have the sort of intelligence required to set up the political and social institutions essential to controlling military technology. So far as I can see, we are drifting toward disaster not because politicians are either ignorant or want this to happen, but because of Man's very nature.

The main, perhaps the only, hope for the future is that the public will learn the facts in time and that an aroused public opinion will force reluctant politicians to stop the nuclear arms race and reduce armaments. I am convinced that political leaders, left to themselves, will not be able to prevent a nuclear holocaust, even though they may sincerely wish to do so. I am equally convinced that if the public knew the truth about the nuclear arms race, it would insist on action by its political leaders to stop this insanity. We will avoid nuclear disaster only if the public protests in time.

Although public opinion in all countries is important, perhaps the greatest responsibility rests with the smaller powers. These should agree on a comprehensive programme of arms control measures leading to far-reaching nuclear disarmament. This programme, possibly in the form of a treaty, could then be presented at a conference to which all countries are invited. As many countries as possible should be persuaded to sign the treaty or adhere to the programme. The nuclear weapon powers are, of course, unlikely to come to such a conference, or to subscribe to the treaty. But absence at the conference would show the world quite clearly which countries refuse to participate in the disarmament programme. The moral force of this demonstration should not be underestimated: in today's world, the larger powers cannot afford to ignore the opinion of the other powers.

2

Global Militarization

THE previous chapter mentioned that a nuclear world war may well escalate from a future war in some Third World region. The militarization of the Third World, therefore, increases the danger of such a nuclear war. Great power military intervention in Third World countries, such as the Soviet invasion of Afghanistan, and great power demonstrations of military power and threats of the use of force, such as recent US naval activities in the Indian Ocean and Persian Gulf, can inflame already sensitive areas. This in turn will strengthen the hands of those groups within Third World countries who argue for increases in military budgets.

Few countries today, rich or poor, can afford to increase their military spending. Huge amounts are already being spent on military activities. Not only does this lead to increasing global militarization, but it involves an increasing waste of scarce resources with obvious social, economic, and ethical consequence.

Few people realize how steadily military spending has increased since World War II. Or that the Soviet and American economies have been essentially war economies ever since World War II. Or that many Third World countries are increasing their military budgets much faster than they are increasing their GNP. Or how totally out of control the global arms trade is and how this contributes to global militarization. Nor is the irrationality of some of the increases in military spending by some countries, including NATO countries, generally realized. But before going into this, let us consider the resources currently used by the military.

World Military Spending

Military spending in real terms (that is, after taking inflation into account) has increased four-fold since the end of World War II. In 1980, world military expenditure will, in current dollars, amount to over $500,000 million, or about a million dollars a minute. A dynamic feature of world military expenditures over the past 15 or so years is the relatively rapid increase in Third World military spending. It is true that the industrialised countries have always spent much more on the military than countries in the Third World, so that the latter started from a relatively low base. But what the recent surge in Third World military spending means is that the entire planet is becoming militarized.

According to SIPRI estimates, Third World military spending in 1965 was about $44,000 million (measured in 1978 dollars). In 1980, the Third World will spend about $113,000 million (in 1978 dollars) on the military, an increase of about 2.6 times over this period.

China is thought to account for a large fraction of Third World military spending; roughly 40 per cent in 1979. For many years now China has given little useful information about its military spending; most estimates are based on Western intelligence data.

Third World military spending is increasing faster than the gross national product (GNP). From 1965 to 1980, Third World GNP increased (in real terms) about 2 times, military spending about 2.6 times.

Many economists believe that military spending has harmful effects even in developed countries. High military budgets are thought to increase inflation, and therefore unemployment, decrease international trade, worsen the balance of payments, and destabilize exchange rates. And, because of them, less development aid flows from the developed to the developing countries.

But high military spending by Third World countries is thought to be directly harmful. There is usually a large difference between spending on the military and on social services. According to Ruth Leger Sivard, an American expert on world military and social expenditures, the average developing country spent in 1976 $18 *per capita* on education, $7 *per capita* on health, and $26 *per capita* on the military. Yet the 3000 million people in the Third World have a life expectancy of about 55 years; on average only about 47 per cent of the school-age population is at school; about a half of the adult population is illiterate; 44 million children under 15 years of age are working; the infant mortality rate is 111 per thousand live births; and 60 per cent of the population has no access to safe water.

But let us go back to the situation in the rich countries. In spite of many differences, it is reasonable to assume that NATO and Warsaw Pact forces are in general about equal, in the sense that in a war it is difficult to predict which side would gain an advantage. Moreover, there is so much military power on each side that quite large differences are meaningless in military terms.

There is, therefore, little, if any, sense in arguments for increases in NATO military spending, at least from a military point of view. The US defence budget for fiscal year 1981, for example, proposes outlays that are 3.3 per cent higher in real terms, after inflation, than in fiscal year 1980. This meets the NATO goal of a 3 per cent real increase in annual defence spending, but will require the diversion of nearly 6 per cent of the American gross national product to military activities. At a time of high inflation and increasing unemployment this is not a sensible use of a nation's resources, particularly since it will give no military advantage over the adversary.

It makes even less sense for Britain to increase its military spending by 3 per cent per year in real terms, as it plans to do, when it is in such dire economic straits that it has to cut savagely spending on the social services. Such absurdity is hard to understand.

Chancellor Schmidt's government, under pressure from his opposition opponent Strauss, also plans to meet the NATO target of 3 per cent by, among other things, increasing defence aid to Turkey. The Federal Republic is better able than most to afford extra military costs.

Belgium and Denmark, however, are going to fall short of a 3 per cent real increase in military spending in 1980. In Belgium the increase will be less than 2 per cent and in Denmark there will be no increase at all. This could lead to reductions in the military forces of these two countries and particularly to economies in the military use of fuel. But to suggest that the decreases will seriously undermine NATO's strength relative to the Warsaw Pact is ridiculous.

In this context it is sensible to ask—what are, in fact, the most serious threats to the West's democratic way of life? In my opinion, the coming economic crisis brought on by a shortage of energy supplies is at least as great a threat as the Warsaw Pact, and probably a much bigger threat. This is particularly so because the Eastern European countries, including the USSR, will be as preoccupied with energy problems as we will be in the West.

The most likely outcome of the energy crisis is, therefore, that economic growth will be very low, perhaps zero or even negative. This will mean much unemployment and probably high inflation.

In these circumstances, increasingly high levels of military spending do more harm than good. For example, they themselves contribute significantly to unemployment and inflation. And they have a cumulative effect, so that military spending in one year affects economic growth for many following years. An American economist, Marion Anderson, has estimated that every billion dollars spent by the US military results in a net loss of 30,000 jobs compared with spending the money for civil purposes. Provided that cuts in military spending were offset by an increase in government spending in other areas or by a tax reduction, then the number of jobs would increase.

To sum up, increases in military spending will not increase the security of NATO countries. On the contrary, a decrease in military budgets could, by increasing employment and reducing inflation, offset to some extent the impact of the coming energy crisis. This would improve the chances of Western democratic societies surviving the stresses and strains caused by the energy crisis. To put it bluntly, we would be more secure if we spent less on the military.

The notion that NATO is militarily weaker than the Warsaw Pact is insupportable. Given the superiority of American military technology compared with Soviet technology, the fact that in a war or crisis many Soviet troops may well be occupied dealing with opposition in Eastern European countries, and the probable unreliability of many Eastern European troops, the greatest military strength is probably on the Western side.

The Arms Trade

The 170 or so wars fought in the Third World since World War II killed more than 30 million people. Most of the weapons used in these wars were supplied through the international arms trade.

The arms trade has increased dramatically and is now virtually out of control. According to SIPRI, the value of exports of major arms (aircraft, armoured vehicles, missiles, and ships) in 1979 was 500 per cent higher than in 1969 and 1200 per cent higher than in 1959.

The arms business is one of the world's most lucrative activities. Global production of military equipment now amounts to $120,000 million a year—ten times the global market for micro-electronics. The arms trade accounts for at least 25 per cent of the turnover, and probably considerably more.

During the 1970s, about 75 per cent of the arms trade was with the Third World. Of this, about 50 per cent went to the Middle East and 25 per cent to Asia. The United States accounted for 45 per cent of the supply, the Soviet Union for 27 per cent, France for 10 per cent and the UK for 5 per cent.

The number of countries producing their own weapons continues to increase. Today, 56 countries produce major weapons; 24 are in the Third World. If small arms are included, then the number of weapon-producing countries is, of course, much larger.

Some Third World weapon producers—notably Israel, South Africa, Brazil, Argentina and India—already compete in the global arms trade.

Some governments use the arms trade to gain political or economic influence, or military bases, in Third World regions. Others believe that selling weapons helps their economies, especially in a recession. Some seek the economies of scale to be had from long production runs. And some want to recover some of the enormous research and development costs involved in modern weapon design. Commercial firms use their considerable influence to persuade their governments to grant them export licences. For these reasons, it would be exceedingly difficult to control the arms trade, even if international relations were cordial.

Controlling the global arms trade is a vital international task. It is through the arms trade that the great powers are likely to become involved in Third World conflicts. If they supply the conventional weapons for a conflict they are likely to be asked to send munitions to replace those used in battle. The 1973 Middle East war showed how rapidly munitions are used in modern war. If new supplies are not quickly sent by the supplier to its client state, then the latter may lose the war. In this way the great power supplier becomes the guarantor of the survival of its client. And, of course, in these days of alliances neither superpower can afford to be seen letting down a recipient of its arms. If it did so, its alliances would be severely weakened. Superpower involvement in a future conventional Third World could escalate to a nuclear world war. Given the frequency of Third World conflicts—one begins on average every three months—there is a very high probability that such escalation will occur.

3

The Spread of Nuclear Weapons

THE escalation of a Third World conflict to a nuclear world war is more likely if the countries fighting the original war use nuclear weapons which they themselves have produced. This chapter will discuss nuclear weapon proliferation.

Unfortunately, some countries are exporting nuclear equipment and material for narrow commercial reasons without much regard for the danger that the equipment and material may assist the importer to make nuclear weapons. There is, in fact, much money involved in the nuclear market—the business has become a multi-billion dollar one. Eight or nine significant national nuclear industries have been established in Japan, Europe, and North America. These are competing for exports in a cut-throat way, because most domestic markets are too small to sustain a national industry without massive government subsidy.

Every ruse is used to secure a deal, including the giving of loans at very low interest rates, relatively easy safeguards arrangements, and so on. And, until recently, countries were prepared to export even the most sensitive elements of the nuclear fuel elements, such as reprocessing plants and uranium-enrichment plants.

The West Germans, for example, sold a reprocessing plant and an enrichment plant to Brazil, along with a number of nuclear power reactors, in a deal worth several billion dollars. The Americans tried hard to dissuade the West Germans from making this sale, but failed to do so. Many believe that a (if not the) main reason for Brazil's interest in nuclear energy is the acquisition of a nuclear weapon option. But Brazil is not the only country with such ambitions. Why do countries want nuclear weapons?

Countries may go nuclear for a variety of reasons. The most important are to solve real or perceived security needs and prestige. There is also likely to be a "domino effect" in some regions: if one country acquires nuclear weapons, then neighbouring ones will feel obliged to follow suit. Pakistan, for example, the next most likely country to explode a nuclear device, will probably do so because of India's nuclear explosion.

Countries like Israel, which most people assume, on rather scant evidence, has a dozen or so nuclear weapons, have or believe they have security problems which they think may be helped by the acquisition of nuclear weapons. Taiwan and South Korea are examples of countries which may eventually acquire nuclear weapons for this reason.

Prestige is an important stimulant for nuclear weapon proliferation. The fact that all the permanent members of the UN Security Council have nuclear weapons is not lost on the non-nuclear weapon powers. Brazil is an example of a country which may acquire nuclear weapons for prestige reasons, to enhance its pre-eminence in Latin America. And if Brazil does so, Argentina will probably feel obliged to follow suit.

Political leaders may want nuclear weapons for internal political reasons—to boost their domestic prestige, or to distract the attention of the population from internal social or economic problems. India may have exploded its nuclear device partly for this reason, partly to impress Pakistan, and partly to try to enhance its security against China.

Some people believe that South Africa has nuclear weapons. The United States and Russia believe that, by political and diplomatic pressures, they stopped South Africa from testing a nuclear device in the Kalahari desert in 1977. But South Africa (or Israel?) may have exploded a nuclear device over the Indian Ocean in 1979; the evidence is still inconclusive.

The use of nuclear weapons in Southern Africa would make no military, or any other, sense, although some diehard fanatics may argue for it as a last ditch effort. But Soviet and American policies towards South Africa, whether based on influencing events directly or by proxy, will be affected by the presence of nuclear weapons. The South African régime may imagine that the threat to use nuclear weapons may in the future provoke the Americans to support it out of fear that such use may escalate to a nuclear world war.

South Korea and Taiwan may by now have been well on the way to producing nuclear weapons if it had not been for American political pressures—in particular, to prevent them reprocessing reactor fuel on a significant scale.

Similar pressures failed in the case of Pakistan, which is reported to be in the final stages of completing a uranium enrichment plant, presumably to produce fissile materials for nuclear weapons. Much of the expertise which has gone into Pakistan's enrichment effort is said to have been acquired by a Pakistani technologist working at the enrichment plant owned by URENCO in The Netherlands.

Even though American pressures failed to prevent the West German sale to Brazil of enrichment and reprocessing facilities, they succeeded in stopping the French sale of a reprocessing plant to Pakistan. Recent reports suggest, however, that the Pakistanis are building a reprocessing plant with some French help. And sales of nuclear equipment to Iraq by France and Italy have not been stopped.

Although we all know that China, France, the UK, the USA, and the USSR have nuclear weapons, we cannot be sure which other countries have them. In fact, all of the non-nuclear weapon countries (whichever they are!) mentioned above could so rapidly produce nuclear weapons, if they chose to do so, that for all political intents and purposes they should be regarded as nuclear weapon powers. Most of these countries (Argentina, Brazil, India, Israel, Pakistan, and South Africa), as well as two nuclear weapon powers (China and France), have not ratified the 1970 Non-Proliferation Treaty (NPT), and therein lies the main weakness of the Treaty. (There are, of course, other non-ratifiers—like Cuba and Egypt—which, some suspect, are interested in peaceful nuclear technology, partly at least to obtain a nuclear weapon option. Some countries—like Iraq, Libya, South Korea, and Taiwan—who have ratified the NPT are suspected of having similar motives for developing nuclear technology. In fact, any country with a significant nuclear programme could rather rapidly produce nuclear weapons, clandestinely if it so wished.

The following countries are the top ten in the list of potential nuclear weapon powers because of perceived or real security needs, prestige, and technological capabilities. Countries with a § are parties to the NPT but, nevertheless, many think that their main interest in nuclear energy is to obtain the option to acquire nuclear weapons.

1. Argentina	6. Libya§
2. Brazil	7. Pakistan
3. Egypt	8. South Africa
4. Iraq§	9. South Korea§
5. Israel	10. Taiwan§

Governmental Nuclear Weapon Proliferation

The fuel in a nuclear reactor is normally uranium, a widely distributed element. As uranium is used up in a nuclear reactor, plutonium—an element not found in nature—is produced as an inevitable by-product. One isotope of plutonium, plutonium-239, readily undergoes fission (like uranium-235) and therein lies the importance of plutonium for fuelling breeder reactors and making nuclear explosives. Plutonium is, in fact, an extremely potent explosive. The energy released by the complete fissioning of one kilogram of plutonium—about the size of a golf ball—would produce an explosion equal to that obtained from about 20,000 tons of TNT (20 kt). An explosion of this magnitude would obliterate a small city. In an atomic bomb of modest efficiency, about 20 per cent of the plutonium is detonated to give a yield of about 20 kt for 5 kg of plutonium (smaller than a grapefruit).

For efficient atomic bombs, plutonium rich, the isotope plutonium-239 is required. Preferably, the proportion of plutonium-239 should exceed 93 per cent. Such plutonium can be obtained from a nuclear power reactor normally used to generate electricity only by severely limiting the burn-up of the uranium fuel—that is, the amount of energy released by the uranium. The fuel elements would have to be removed from the reactor after a period of only a few weeks instead of the normal period of between 3 and 4 years. This operation would be a nuisance for the reactor operator and difficult to do clandestinely, particularly since this would have to be done repeatedly if a stockpile of atomic bombs were required. At least some of the power station staff would know that something unusual was afoot.

Plutonium *could* also be obtained clandestinely from a plutonium production reactor, acquired specially for the purpose. A small reactor with a power of about 40 megawatts of electricity could produce enough plutonium-239 annually for two 20-kt atomic bombs. The components for such a small reactor can be easily, and secretly, obtained on the open market for a cost of less than $20 million. The reactor and a small chemical reprocessing unit to remove the plutonium from the reactor fuel elements could be clandestinely constructed and run by, say, the military.

Uranium enriched to more than about 40 per cent uranium-235 can also be used to construct nuclear weapons. As the case of Pakistan shows, a small uranium enrichment plant can be constructed specifically to produce fissile material for nuclear weapons. South Africa has also built a pilot enrichment plant which could have provided material for nuclear weapons.

The possession of one or more nuclear power reactors and access to a commercial reprocessing plant, or the possession of a uranium enrichment plant, is often regarded as the essential prerequisite for a country wishing to produce nuclear weapons.

This explains the current concern about the acquisition of nuclear power reactors, and more particularly of reprocessing or enrichment plants, by new countries which do not now have nuclear weapons.

The Safeguards Problem

A typical commercial reprocessing plant may reprocess about 12,000 kg of plutonium a year. Perhaps 3000 kg or so would be in store at any one time. A nuclear weapon of the type which destroyed Nagasaki could be made using a few kilograms of plutonium.

The present systems for safeguarding plutonium, such as those developed by the International Atomic Energy Agency (IAEA) and Euratom, are based on material accounting and material control and are simply not able to give a high enough assurance that significant quantities of plutonium have not been removed from a commercial reprocessing plant to satisfy a reasonably cautious man. It must be emphasized that this inability to account adequately for the plutonium in a reprocessing plant is not due to the possible misuse or limitations of instruments. Even with the best technology feasible, the task would be impossible. A major problem is that the amount of plutonium in spent reactor fuel elements brought to the reprocessing plant cannot be well enough measured. And very accurate calculations of this amount are not possible. The input of the plant cannot, therefore, be known to a sufficient degree of accuracy.

Adequate protection against the theft or diversion of significant quantities of plutonium from a reprocessing plant would then have to depend mainly on physical protection measures—particularly by limiting human access to the plutonium. This would involve such procedures as the continuous observation of workers handling nuclear material, much searching of employees entering and leaving protected areas, and probably the off-site surveillance of employees.

The magnitude of the task facing those who guard plutonium is illustrated by the fact that a typical packet of twenty cigarettes could hold about 1300 grams of plutonium oxide, the form in which the plutonium normally occurs in a reprocessing plant. Eight such packets could contain enough plutonium for a crude atomic bomb. The necessary technology is not yet available to perform these physical protection tasks. To do so adequately would, in any case, involve high financial investments. And, in the final analysis, the human element sets the limit to the certainty with which the theft or diversion of plutonium can be prevented even if the very best technology is used.

In a democracy it is extremely unlikely that the procedures required to safeguard a large reprocessing plant adequately—i.e. by using physical protection measures—would, even if possible, be socially acceptable.

The Spread of Nuclear Power

Nuclear materials are being produced in an increasing number of countries. So far, a total of 100,000 kg of plutonium has been accumulated from civilian nuclear power reactors. At present, about 230 power reactors are generating about 120,000 megawatts of electricity (MW(e)) in 22 countries; another 230 or so power reactors are under construction. By the year 2000, reactors generating about 600,000 MW(e) may be operational and about 150,000 kg of plutonium produced a year—enough to make roughly 30,000 bombs of the Nagasaki type. The spread of reactor grade plutonium is the most immediate threat to the non-proliferation régime.

For many years it was thought that there are technical possibilities for stopping the proliferation. At the meetings during the International Fuel Cycle Evaluation (INFCE), held from November 1978 until February 1980, it appeared that governments at last realize that only a political solution can stop the spread of nuclear weapons. But until now this solution has not been found. The number of parties to NPT has reached 114, showing that the non-proliferation idea, at least, is widely accepted. But, the non-proliferation régime will be seriously threatened as long as any states with significant nuclear activities remain outside the treaty. There are now as many as about a dozen such states.

Fragile though it is, the NPT is our only barrier to nuclear proliferation, now that the technology of nuclear weapon design is so well known. It is, therefore, essential that we strengthen the treaty as much as we can. The treaty itself allows for periodic opportunities to do this, at conferences of the parties to review its operation. the first review conference was held on 5–30 May 1975: the second was held in Geneva between 11 August and 5 September 1980.

A main complaint of the non-nuclear weapon parties to the NPT is the failure of the nuclear weapon parties—the UK, the USA, and the USSR—to live up to their commitment to pursue negotiations on effective measures of nuclear disarmament.

The Treaty is 10 years old, but we still have neither a SALT II treaty nor a comprehensive test ban, the two measures most needed to show "good faith" on the part of the superpowers towards this disarmament commitment. Worse still, the nuclear arms race is about to accelerate again in a most dangerous direction, with the development and deployment of Soviet and American strategic and tactical nuclear war fighting weapons.

The nuclear weapon parties—particularly the USA and the USSR—are faced with a dilemma. They have proved themselves over the past 30 years incapable of controlling their nuclear arms race. Vertical proliferation is essentially out of political control.

On the other hand, the Russians and Americans realize that the spread of nuclear weapons to other countries—horizontal proliferation—is exceedingly dangerous for them (and, of course, for the world as a whole) because it too increases the probability of a nuclear world war. But how can these powers expect others not to acquire nuclear weapons when they demonstrate, by continually improving the size and quality of their nuclear arsenals, that they believe that nuclear weapons have a high political and military value?

The nuclear weapon powers have to face the international political reality that horizontal proliferation will be controlled only if vertical proliferation is controlled. A start should be made by ratifying SALT II and negotiating a permanent comprehensive test ban treaty.

These measures are necessary but perhaps not sufficient to strengthen adequately the non-proliferation régime. Others are needed:

- Exporting countries party to the NPT should supply nuclear material, equipment, and services to non-parties only if the latter countries accept International Atomic Energy Agency (IAEA) safeguards on *all* their peaceful nuclear activities.
- Non-parties should be persuaded to join the treaty by denying

them supplies of nuclear materials and equipment; outright defiance of the treaty should be dealt with even more stringently.

- Safeguards procedures should be improved, and IAEA authority strengthened, so that any diversion of fissionable material for weapon purposes can be rapidly detected and quick action taken.
- The sensitive parts of the nuclear fuel cycle (particularly, reprocessing and uranium enrichment) should be put under the authority of an international agency and an international repository of spent fuels and a bank of fresh fuels established. In the meantime, nuclear-weapon countries should be discouraged from building their own reprocessing or uranium enrichment plants. Perhaps most important of all, countries wishing to develop and rely on non-nuclear energy sources should be encouraged.

Hopefully, these minimum measures will soon be put into effect. Otherwise, no one can say where horizontal proliferation will stop. A Pakistani bomb would obviously trigger a nuclear arms race with India. And then, Iraq? South Korea? Taiwan? Japan?

Conclusion

These technical measures can only be implemented when the situation improves in the political field; the NPT must grow into a stronger institution, in order to slow down, or even prevent, the spread of nuclear weapons. A long-term solution of this problem must also include the resolution of regional security problems, so that states do not perceive the need to develop nuclear weapons for security reasons. Also, the belief that nuclear weapons bring prestige must be eliminated. In summary, then:

- peaceful nuclear programmes make more likely the proliferation of nuclear weapons;
- in particular, the expansion of the nuclear fuel cycle, especially the construction of national reprocessing and enrichment plants, increases the probability that new countries will acquire nuclear weapons; such proliferation increases the danger of a nuclear world war.

It is particularly important to stress that:

- the plutonium produced in a nuclear power reactor operated normally is suitable for use as the fissile material in an effective atomic bomb; this plutonium is more hazardous to people handling it than weapons grade plutonium, but not greatly so; plutonium oxide, the form in which plutonium may be taken from a reprocessing plant, can be handled without extraordinary precautions;
- a nuclear explosive device made from reactor plutonium need not be likely to explode prematurely; a nuclear explosion based on a relatively simple design, like the Nagasaki one, and using a reactor grade plutonium, would explode with a power equivalent to that of at least 1000 tons of TNT; and a nuclear explosion equivalent to that of a few hundred tons of TNT can do a great deal of damage and kill many people if it took place in an urban area.

4

The Nuclear Weapons That Are in Use

IN this chapter I discuss some aspects of the nuclear arms race. I do not pretend to give a complete overview of all the weapons that are deployed.

The greatest single threat to humankind is undoubtedly the nuclear arsenals of the superpowers. These are, by any standards, enormous.

American *strategic* nuclear forces carry about 9200 nuclear warheads, with a total explosive power equivalent to that of about 4,000 million tonnes of high explosive. Soviet strategic nuclear forces could deliver about 5000 nuclear warheads, with a total explosive power equivalent to that of about 7500 million tonnes of high explosive. In the tactical nuclear arsenals there are said to be several tens of thousands of nuclear warheads, each on average several times more powerful than the Hiroshima bomb. These add another 4500 or so million tonnes of high explosive equivalent to make a total of about 16,000 million tonnes—the equivalent of about 1,250,000 Hiroshima bombs.

A nuclear world war in which a significant fraction of those weapons were used would almost certainly destroy all the major cities in the Northern Hemisphere (there are only about 400 of these, *each* on average targeted with the equivalent of roughly 20 million tonnes of TNT or more than all explosives used in all the wars in history); kill the bulk of the urban population in the Northern Hemisphere by blast and fire, and the bulk of the rural population by radiation.

The need to limit and then drastically reduce the nuclear arsenals is obvious. The SALT II agreement signed by President Carter and President Brezhnev on 18th June, 1979 in Vienna is meant to be a step in this direction. But on 3 January 1980 President Carter requested the US Senate to postpone the debate on the SALT II Treaty "in the light of the Soviet invasion of Afghanistan". Without the SALT II Treaty, it is extremely unlikely that there will be significant progress in the negotiation of any other arms control treaty—in particular a comprehensive nuclear test ban or a ban on chemical weapons.

From an international political point of view, and for the sake of progress in arms control and disarmament, the importance of SALT II cannot be overestimated and the treaty should, therefore, be ratified as soon as possible. In the meantime, it is to be hoped that both sides will continue to comply with the provisions of the SALT II Treaty.

The SALT II Treaty

The agreement has three components: a treaty lasting until the end of 1985; a protocol that runs until the end of 1981; and a joint statement of principles and guidelines for subsequent SALT negotiations. Also included are a commitment by the USSR about the Soviet Backfire Bomber and a memorandum listing the numbers of strategic weapons deployed by both sides in various categories as of 18 June 1979.

An initial limit of 2400 strategic delivery systems—intercontinental ballistic missile (ICBM) launchers, submarine-launched ballistic missile (SLBM) launchers, long-range bombers, and air-to-surface ballistic missiles (ASBM) with ranges over 600 km—allowed to each side is to be reduced to 2250 by 31 December 1981. ICBMs are defined as land-based ballistic missiles with a range in excess of 5500 km. So far, neither country has deployed ASBMs (ballistic missiles launched from an aircraft against a target on the Earth's surface).

The United States now has 1710 ballistic missiles (1054 ICBMs and 656 SLBMs) of which 1046 (550 ICBMs and 496 SLBMs) are

SALT II limits and US and Soviet strategic nuclear forces as of 18 June 1979

SALT II limits		USA	USSR
2250 / (MIRV) 1320 / 1200 / 820	MIRVed ICBM launchers	550	608
2250 / (MIRV) 1320 / 1200	MIRVed SLBM launchers	496	144
2250 / (MIRV) 1320	Heavy bombers equipped for long-range ALCMs	3	0
2250	Non-MIRVed ICBM launchers	504	790
2250	Non-MIRVed SLBM launchers	160	806
2250	Heavy bombers not equipped for long-range ALCMs	570	156
	Total	2283	2504

Total systems by development category

	USA	USSR
ICBM launchers	1054	1398
SLBM launchers	656	950
Heavy bombers	573	156
Total	2283	2504

Key: ALCM (air-launched cruise missile)
ICBM (intercontinental ballistic missile)
MIRV (multiple independently targetable re-entry vehicle)
SLBM (submarine-launched ballistic missile)

MIRVed. Some 300 B52s are operational as long-range strategic bombers. Under the new agreement the USA will have to dismantle 36 strategic delivery systems (presumably mothballed B-52s).

The Soviet Union has deployed 2348 ballistic missiles (1398 ICBMs and 950 SLBMs), of which about 752 (608 ICBMs and 144 SLBMs) are MIRVed. About 140 of its long-range bombers are probably assigned strategic roles. Under the new agreement, the USSR will have to dismantle 254 strategic delivery systems. These will presumably be obsolete ones.

The total of about 14,000 strategic nuclear warheads which may be deployed by the end of 1985 (despite SALT II) represents a significant increase in the size of the US nuclear arsenal. Similarly, the number of warheads in the Soviet nuclear arsenals is likely to increase considerably, mainly because of the deployment of more MIRVed SLBMs. The new agreement is, therefore, hardly a significant disarmament measure, even though 300 or so obsolete strategic delivery systems will have to be dismantled.

Qualitative developments in strategic nuclear weapons are more likely to increase the probability of a nuclear world war than are increases in numbers of warheads. For some time now these numbers have been so huge that further increases have had no military or strategic significance. Both the USA and the USSR, however, are improving their nuclear weapons, particularly the accuracy and reliability of ballistic missile warheads.

The SALT Treaty does place some qualitative restrictions on the development and deployment of new types of nuclear weapons. But these are relatively minor. SLBMs are restricted to no more than 14 warheads each, the maximum number so far tested by either side.

The treaty contains several provisions helping each side to verify that the other is complying with the agreements. For example, it is difficult to distinguish between MIRVed and non-MIRVed missiles once they have been deployed. The treaty thus specifies that all missiles of a type that has been tested with MIRVs shall be counted as MIRVed, even if deployed with a single warhead. All launchers of a type that has contained or launched MIRVed missiles are counted as MIRVed.

Because the Soviet SS-16, a mobile ICBM, is similar enough to the SS-20 intermediate range ballistic missile to complicate verification, the USSR has agreed not to deploy or test SS-16s, or to produce more of them. And there is to be an exchange of data on the numbers and characteristics of strategic weapon systems limited by the SALT Treaty. Given the Soviet habit of extreme secrecy about strategic (and other) weapons, this exchange is a considerable step forward.

The treaty explicitly states that verification will be by "national technical means". This includes satellites (particularly photo reconnaissance satellites), ground-based systems (such as radars which observe missile tests and antennas which collect telemetry), and aircraft based systems (including optical and other sensors). Deliberate concealment activities which impede verification are prohibited. Specifically, any telemetry encryption (the encoding of missile test data) which hampers verification is banned. So is interference with the other side's intelligence collection systems.

The SALT II protocol, which expires on 31 December 1981, places temporary limits on certain contentious weapons. It bans the deployment of mobile ICBM launchers and the flight testing of mobile ICBMs. none of these restrictions significantly affects current plans for the development or deployment of ballistic or cruise missiles.

In early June, just before going to Vienna to sign the SALT Treaty, President Carter authorized the full-scale development (but not the deployment) of a new ICBM, the M-X mobile missile. This will presumably be the American choice for the one new type of ICBM allowed by the SALT II Treaty.

Loop road for one missile with 23 shelters

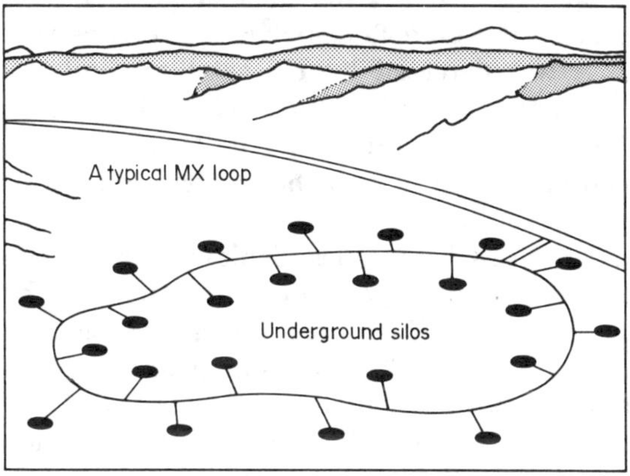

Advocates for the M-X argue that Soviet ICBMs are, or soon will be, accurate enough to destroy American fixed land-based ICBMs in their hardened silos. If this is so, then one might think that the obvious thing to do is to do away with land-based ICBMs and rely instead on SLBMs which, for a while at least, will remain relatively invulnerable. But, sensible though this may be, the US Air Force, the service responsible for American ICBMs, is most unwilling to give them up mainly because it would then have a much less powerful voice in strategic affairs. Its rival, the US Navy, would have correspondingly more influence. Inter-service rivalry is much more likely to determine events than considerations of national, let alone world, security. Given the power of the US Air Force's political lobby, we must expect land-based ICBMs to be with us for the foreseeable future. The M-X missile, by design, will fit into the existing Minuteman silos. But, if deployed, a mobile basing system will almost certainly be used. Currently, the most likely basing scheme is the horizontal shelter one in which the missiles would be moved between hardened shelters on a transporter–erector–launcher vehicle. Each MX would be moved along a road, or around a loop of roadway. If the transporter, possibly a 450,000 kg vehicle, travelled along the road at an appropriate speed, the missile could be moved to any one of the hardened shelters along the road in the 30 minutes or so it would take between the time the launch of Soviet ICBMs was detected by US satellites and the time the warheads detonated in the USA. The M-X missiles could, therefore, be moved after the Soviet ICBMs were launched. The Soviets would have to attack all the shelters to be sure of hitting the missiles.

The number of M-X missiles deployed and the number of shelters per missile will depend on perceptions of the potential Soviet threat to the US ICBM force. The most often cited numbers are 200 M-Xs and about 8000 aim points. The cost of the system will depend on the basing mode but will be at least $30,000 million and may exceed $100,000 million. The M-X schedule calls for a flight test in 1983. If deployed, the first missiles could be operational in 1986.

If SALT II is not ratified, there could be an open-ended arms race between the number of M-X missiles deployed by the Americans and the number of warheads deployed by the Russians to counter them. The limits imposed by SALT II would at least prohibit this particular spiral of the arms race.

Submarines

The Soviet and American navies operate a total of 113 modern strategic nuclear submarines —the USSR has 72 and the USA 41. The ballistic missiles carried by these submarines are normally targeted on the adversary's cities to provide the assured destruction on which nuclear deterrence depends. A single modern US strategic nuclear submarine, for example, carries about 200 nuclear warheads, enough to destroy every Soviet city with a population of more than 150,000. American cities are hostages to Soviet strategic nuclear submarines to a similar extent.

The quality of strategic nuclear submarines and the ballistic missiles they carry is being continuously improved.

According to current plans, 14 Trident submarines will become operational during the 1980s, at a rate of three every two years. But the ultimate size of the Trident fleet has yet to be decided.

Trident submarines are extremely expensive—each costs nearly $2000 million. The complete Trident programme, as currently conceived, is likely to cost well over $30,000 million.

The Trident is by far the world's biggest submarine. It is 171 m long, has a maximum hull diameter of 12.8 m, and displaces 18,700 tons when submerged. The enormous size of the Trident can be judged from the facts that it is twice as large as a Polaris/Poseidon submarine, which has a submerged displacement of about 8300 tons, and is as large as the new British through-deck cruiser (displacement 19,500 tons).

The Trident submarine will carry a crew of 164. Two crews will be provided for every submarine. Each crew will do a 70-day patrol. The patrol period is limited by the stamina of the crew rather than by the endurance of the submarine.

Each Trident will carry 24 SLBMs. The Trident I SLBM is designed to have a maximum range of 4000 nautical miles (7400 km) when equipped with eight 100-kiloton (kT) MIRVed warheads. Even longer ranges can be achieved if the missile has a smaller payload. The Poseidon SLBM, which it replaces, can carry up to fourteen 40-kT MIRVed warheads, but has a maximum range of only 2500 nautical miles (4600 km). With the longer range missile, Trident submarines will be able to operate in 16 times more ocean area and still remain within range of its targets. The long-range missiles will also allow Trident submarines to operate closer to American shores and still reach their targets, giving the submarines greater protection against Soviet ASW activities.

The CEP of the Trident I SLBM is probably about 500 m at maximum rage, whereas that of the Poseidon SLBM is about 550 m, and that of the Polaris I SLBM about 900m.

SLBM warheads may eventually be fitted with terminal guidance, using radar, a laser, or some other device to guide them onto their targets after re-entry into the Earth's atmosphere. This could give CEPs of a few tens of metres. SLBMs will then be so accurate as to cease to be only countercity weapons and become counterforce weapons able to threaten even relatively small military targets. If deployed, the Trident II SLBM will be such a counterforce weapon.

Almost all Soviet strategic nuclear warheads are deployed on ballistic missiles; it operates no more than 150 strategic bombers. There are said to be about 5000 independently targetable Soviet missile warheads. Of these, about 1200, or 24 per cent, are probably carried by SLBMs. The rest are on ICBMs. The SLBM warheads probably have a total explosive yield of about 900 Mt, about 13 per cent of the total explosive yield of Soviet missile warheads. According to US sources, the Soviet Union normally has only about one-seventh of its strategic submarines (about ten boats) at sea at any one time. The land-based ICBM force is, at present, therefore, by far the most important component of the Soviet strategic nuclear arsenal. The threat to the land-based missile posed by very accurate ICBMs is far more serious to the USSR than to the USA.

The most modern Soviet SLBM is the 4000 nautical mile (7400 km) range SS-N-18, equipped with three 200-kT MIRVs. So far, 144 SS-N-18s have been deployed, 16 on each of 9 Delta-class submarines, the most modern Soviet strategic nuclear submarines. The other main Soviet SLBM is the SS-N-8, with a range of 4300 nautical miles (7950 km) and a single 1-Mt warhead. Two hundred and sixty-eight SS-N-8s are deployed on 21 Delta-class submarines.

Soviet strategic nuclear submarines are, generally speaking, technologically inferior to their American counterparts, mainly because they are much noisier and, therefore, easier to detect by ASW systems. Moreover, Soviet SLBMs are much less accurate than American ones.

Anti-submarine Warfare

A very large effort is being put into improving ASW techniques by both the USA and the USSR.

According to the 1979 SIPRI Yearbook, American ASW is ahead of Soviet ASW in that it could already seriously limit the damage which would be done by the Soviet strategic ballistic missile submarine fleet in a second strike. For one thing, if in the rather unlikely, but not impossible, event, that the Americans could attack without any warning, probably only about 10 Soviet strategic submarines would be at sea. And an exceedingly powerful American ASW force could be ranged against these 10 boats. The Soviet submarines in port would be relatively easy to destroy.

The Soviet submarine fleet is, in any case, much disadvantaged by geography. Its exits to the Atlantic and Pacific oceans are narrow enough channels to be relatively easily monitored by existing ASW equipment. ASW barriers have, in fact, been established in the Greenland–Iceland–UK gap, in the various Japanese Straits, and off the Aleutians.

In ASW, detection remains the critical element. Detection methods are being improved by increasing the sensitivity of sensors, improving the integration between various sensing systems, and better processing of data from sensors. All types of ASW sensors are being improved—electromagnetic ones, based on radar, infrared, lasers and optics; acoustic ones, including active and passive sonar; and magnetic ones, in which the magnetic field disturbance caused by a submarine is measured. Airborne, spaceborne, ocean–surface, and sea-bottom sensors are being increasingly integrated and, therefore, made more effective. ASW aircraft, surface ships, and hunter killer submarines are also being made increasingly complementary. Each system has special characteristics and the integration of those that complement each other greatly enhances overall effectiveness.

A typical US ASW task force would employ an ASW carrier equipped with specialized aircraft, destroyers equipped with ASW helicopters, and attack submarines. The task force would cooperate with land-based aircraft and receive information from unmanned surveillance systems—all to hunt down and destroy a single enemy strategic nuclear submarine. Once detected, the submarine would be relatively easy to destroy. The enemy submarine would be attacked by torpedoes, missiles, depth charges and mines.

Soviet ASW is based mainly on naval helicopter carriers and long-range, land-based aircraft. Three Soviet helicopter carriers are in service, mainly intended for fleet defence. Search helicopters carry very sophisticated electronic equipment to detect and track enemy submarines. Armed helicopters destroy them. The USSR also operates a number of ASW cruisers and destroyers.

Several types of Soviet long-range aircraft—the latest being the Tu-22M "Backfire"—equipped with the most modern high-resolution radar and magnetic anomaly detection equipment, are designed to detect and destroy US strategic submarines. Soviet ASW activities tend to be much more short range than US ASW activities and largely confined to areas close to Soviet territory or Soviet fleets.

The USA and USSR each operate hunter killer fleets, several dozen boats strong. A hunter-killer is designed to find and then follow an enemy strategic submarine until it is ordered to destroy it.

Cruise Missiles

The US strategic bomber force, the third component of the American strategic triad, will be modernized by equipping B-52 strategic bombers with air-launched cruise missiles (ALCMs). The ALCM is a small, long-range, very accurate, nuclear armed, winged vehicle.

According to current plans, ALCMs should become operational in December 1982, when the first B-52G squadron is loaded with cruise missiles under the aircrafts' wings. Full operational capability is planned for 1990, when all 151 B-52G aircraft will be loaded, each with 12 ALCMs under the wings and 8 in the bomb bays. ALCMs will about double the number of nuclear weapons these aircraft carry.

The Soviet Union is considerably behind the USA in modern

cruise missile development. This is mainly because cruise missiles depend on the miniaturization of electronic components for the guidance system of the missiles. The US is far ahead of the USSR in electronic microminiaturization technology.

Other Strategic Nuclear Forces

The UK, France, and China have also deployed strategic forces, although the number of weapons involved (a total of 1000 or so) is small compared with the number deployed by the USA and the USSR. The UK maintains four strategic nuclear-powered submarines, armed with a total of 64 Polaris A-3 missiles, and a fleet of 56 Vulcan bombers. The UK is considering replacing its strategic nuclear submarines and the missiles carried by these submarines, and will soon retire the Vulcans.

France also has five strategic nuclear submarines equipped with 64 M-2 or M-20 missiles, and plans to build another submarine. France will modernize its SLBM forces with a new warhead which has a limited MIRV capability. France also deploys 18 land-based intermediate range ballistic missiles, and 33 Mirage IVA aircraft are assigned a strategic nuclear role.

According to US sources, China currently deploys three types of liquid fuel ballistic missiles: about 50 short-range missiles with a range of about 1000 km, about 60 intermediate-range missiles with a range of around 2500 km, and 2 intercontinental missiles with a maximum range of 7000 km. China has, in addition, over 100 TU-16 (Badger) medium-range bombers with an operational radius of about 2000 km. China is developing a liquid fuel ICBM with a range estimated at over 10,000 km. Missiles with this range were tested in May 1980.

The British, French, and Chinese nuclear forces are very small compared to those of the Americans and Russians, probably amounting, all told, to about 1500 nuclear warheads including tactical ones. Nevertheless, each of these "small" nuclear forces could wreak unimaginable damage.

The Increasing Danger of a Nuclear World War

The atomic bomb which destroyed Hiroshima had a physical weight of about 4 tons and an explosive yield of about 12.5 kT. The accuracy with which the Hiroshima bomb was dropped depended on the eyesight of the bomb-aimer in the B-29 bomber that delivered the weapon. Nuclear warheads will soon be deliverable with a CEP of about 100 m at a range of 10,000 km.

In a mere 30 years, military technology has produced, from scratch, the ultimate in the design of nuclear warheads and land-based ballistic missiles.

Further into the future we can expect the development of space-based systems for destroying ballistic missiles in flight. High-energy lasers and heavy particle beams are already being studied for this purpose.

As these offensive and defensive strategic weapon systems are deployed, so the profitability of a nuclear world war will increase.

All these systems carry a great danger: the *mere possession* of many types of accurate destruction methods encourage the use of one or some of them.

5

From Nuclear Deterrence to Nuclear War Fighting

MANY strategic nuclear weapons (probably more than a half) have for many years been aimed at military targets, albeit large ones often in or close to cities. Nevertheless, the official nuclear policy (at least in the USA) has been based on mutual assured destruction with the opponent's cities as the hostages. But nuclear policies are now increasingly emphasizing nuclear war fighting (or counterforce) strategies. This is not because the requirements for nuclear deterrence have changed, but because military technology has made counterforce weapons available. Once available, weapons are most often deployed. Policies are then modified to rationalize this deployment.

It must be stressed that neither American nor Soviet politicians have ordered the manufacture of nuclear war fighting weapons for some political purpose; it is uncontrolled military technology which has made the weapons available.

A nuclear world war is increasingly likely as the two superpowers come to rely on counterforce strategies and as the credibility of nuclear deterrence decreases. Nuclear deterrence by mutual assured destruction requires that each side can absorb a surprise nuclear attack and still have sufficient strategic nuclear forces left to do "unacceptable damage" to the attacker's cities and industries. The deployment of very accurate missiles and effective anti-submarine warfare could enable one side to destroy so much of the opponent's retaliatory forces that he would no longer be able to deter effectively an attack.

In this context, a successful first strike need not mean the ability to destroy all of the enemy's retaliatory forces. It is sufficient if one side *perceives* that it has the capability of destroying enough of the other side's retaliatory forces so as to limit the casualties and damage it would suffer from a retaliatory strike to an "acceptable" level for a given political goal. The more reckless the political and military leaders are, the higher this level will be.

It should be pointed out that the fact that the long-term effects may be much more serious than the short-term ones is not likely to be taken into account by leaders when they consider nuclear war. Experience shows that just because these effects are unpredictable, and long-term, they are likely to be ignored.

Foreseeable advances in military technology, of the type described above, may well cause the following events. One day, perhaps towards the end of this decade, the Chairman of the US Joint Chiefs of Staff walks into the President's office and tells him, quite out of the blue:

> Mr. President, our intelligence agencies tell us that the Russians will soon be able to deliver a disabling first strike against us. They could by a surprise attack so reduce our strategic forces that we will be able to kill, in a retaliatory strike, only twenty or thirty million of their people. And remember, Mr. President, [the Chairman goes on] the Russians were able to take such losses in World War II. You know how much effort they have recently put into civil defense. Much of their industry is protected from nuclear blast. If we don't attack them while we have the chance, they will probably attack us soon. If we strike first now, we will keep our casualties from their return strike down to twenty or thirty million. Our own civil defense effort over the past eight years has been quite successful, you know. I know that twenty million dead is horrible enough, but, believe me, if we wait until they hit us first we will lose 100 or maybe 150 million people. Mr. President, can we afford to wait?

This argument will, if ever made, be faulty because, as we have seen, it ignores all but the early deaths from a nuclear war. It is also based on worst case analysis—assuming that the enemy's forces will work according to plan, whereas one's own will work in a much less than optimum way. But we know enough about how military and strategic thinking goes to know that such objections are unlikely to stop the argument from being made. We also know that in such tense situations political leaders are normally much more influenced by their military advisers than by their scientific advisers.

It is very hard to say what an American President, or a Soviet one, in the unlikely event that the Russians forge ahead of the Americans in military technology, would do if faced with this problem. Even the most peace-loving leader would be in an unenviable situation. It would be particularly tricky for him if he were faced with the decision at a time of an international crisis, say a Middle East war, or at a period of exceptionally high tension between East and West. And if the leader were reckless, the situation would be even more dangerous.

If we cannot predict how a future President would act if faced with the need to decide about making a first nuclear strike, we can be sure that if military technology is not controlled he will sooner or later actually have to make the decision.

The Move Away from Nuclear Deterrence based on Mutual Assured Destruction

We know a great deal about American nuclear policies because they are publicly discussed. We know relatively little about Soviet nuclear policies which are rarely discussed in public. What little we do know comes from the writings of a few Soviet military nuclear strategists.

On 29 January 1980 US Secretary of Defense Harold Brown presented his annual report to the US Congress in support of his new military budget application. In it he readily admitted that the use of any nuclear weapon was likely to escalate to a nuclear world war—"avoiding escalation to mutual destruction is not likely". Even so, he argued for the capability to make limited nuclear attacks against the USSR. "For nearly 20 years", he said, "we have explicitly included a range of employment options—against military as well as non-military targets—in our strategic nuclear employment planning."

Current US nuclear policy, as is clear from Secretary Brown's statement, is a muddled mixture of deterrence by mutual assured destruction and nuclear war fighting.

The change in official policy from nuclear deterrence based on mutual assured destruction to nuclear war fighting, or counterforce as it is called, took place in the early 1970s. Typical of the arguments used to support the change are those given in an influential article in the American magazine *Foreign Affairs* in January 1973 written by Fred Iklé, former head of the US Arms Control and Disarmament Agency.

Iklé wrote that the doctrine of mutual assured destruction rests on three dogmas. First, US nuclear forces must be designed almost exclusively for retaliation in response to a Soviet nuclear attack. Second, US forces must be designed and operated in such a way that this retaliation can be swift, massive, and prompt. Third, the threatened retaliation must be the killing of a major fraction of the Soviet population. Moreover, the same ability to decimate the US population must be guaranteed by the Soviet government. Iklé argued that these requirements of stable deterrence are harmful to the prospects of disarmament. His major criticism was that deterrence by mutual assured destruction disregards the very significant possibility of nuclear war breaking out by accident, miscalculation or madness: complete reliance is put into deterring war by "rational" decisions.

Iklé recommended a new strategy in which the potential accuracy of missiles, and current choices in weapon effects, should be used to enable both sides to avoid the killing of millions of civilians and yet to inflict assured destruction on military and industrial targets. He also recommended that strategic forces should be made as invulnerable as possible in order to break the "vicious circle" inherent in the present strategic doctrine, namely, that nuclear forces must be ready for immediate launching because they are vulnerable and that they are vulnerable because they must be ready.

He claimed that these changes, although "avoiding the killing of hostages", would not make nuclear war more acceptable as an instrument of policy. Deterrence would remain effective. In fact, he argued that since the aggressors' conventional military power (the navy, army and air force) and its support facilities would be the first to suffer destruction, it would be even less tempting for the military to plan a nuclear war. And the risk of the destruction of population centres would still exist in the background.

Immediate objections were raised in the USA to the proposals for the adoption of a counterforce strategy. The main arguments against such a strategy are summarized in another *Foreign Affairs* article, published in October 1973, by Wolfgang Panofsky.

While accepting that the present strategic doctrine requires that strategic nuclear forces must be designed primarily for retaliation in response to a nuclear attack, Panofsky denied that this response, according to the present doctrine, need be rapid and massive. He pointed out that a successful first strike against a combination of nuclear forces (submarines, land-based missiles and bombers) is technically impossible at the moment. There is, therefore, no need for a rapid response to a nuclear attack.

Panofsky also pointed out that the destructiveness of the present nuclear arsenals is so great that deaths would number in the tens of millions, even if only a fraction of one side's nuclear weapons were delivered on the opponent's territory. Therefore, even if a nuclear attack were confined to "military" targets, civilian casualties would still be very high. Moreover, it is impossible to be sure that an opponent would follow a similar "antimilitary" strategy. And once the "barriers against use of nuclear weapons are broken, escalation toward full scale war is exceedingly difficult to prevent".

Panofsky concluded that there is no technological way of escaping "the evil dilemma that the strategic forces on both sides must either be designed to kill people or else jeopardize the opponent's confidence in his deterrent".

Similar objections were raised by Herbert York, a former Presidential Science Adviser and high Defense Department official, in a paper presented at a conference held in Washington in October 1973:

> . . . [S]uch counterforce strategies, as they are called, always turn out to require or at least justify, many more and generally larger weapons. . . . In such a case, a failure in deterrence would generally result in many more deaths, especially in third countries, than would be the case for a force sized for deterrence only. This comes about partly due to an increase in collateral damage through fallout, and also because of the colocation of so many military targets with urban targets such as the military command posts in Washington, Omaha and Moscow; the transportation centres in St. Louis, Chicago, Kharkov and Kiev; the naval bases at New York, Boston, San Diego, Los Angeles, Leningrad, Sevastopol and Vladivostock, and so on.
>
> Moreover, a policy to target only military installations would only be an administrative arrangement; it would not rely on anything intrinsic in the equipment. Hence such a policy, agreed to internationally or not, could be abandoned or abrogated on short notice, after first being used to justify a substantial increase in force levels. For these reasons, I believe the proposals for improving the present situation by going to a counterforce strategy are among the most dangerous proposals I know.

In the face of considerable opposition within America, then US Secretary of Defense Schlesinger announced on 10 January 1974 that the USA actually intends to adopt a counterforce strategy as a strategic nuclear option and to this end is improving the accuracy of delivery of its nuclear weapon systems.

In answering the question "Do you think it is possible to have a limited nuclear war, just to exchange a couple of weapons?", the Secretary said: "I believe so." He added: "It is easier to think of the circumstances in which limited use might occur than it would be to think of a massive all-out strike against the urban industrial base of another nation, which has the capability of striking back."

The crux of the matter is that because the officially adopted counterforce strategy makes nuclear war more "flexible", it makes it more thinkable and, therefore, more probable. Moreover, it demands large numbers of accurate weapons, a requirement which triggered off a new round in the strategic nuclear arms race. And few would agree that nuclear war could be kept limited. Any use of nuclear weapons, regardless of type, would almost certainly escalate into an all-out nuclear war.

The debate on nuclear deterrent policies underlines the inherent dilemma produced by the existence of large nuclear arsenals. All nuclear doctrines have severe shortcomings, mainly because they cannot reduce the probability of the use of the weapons to an acceptably low level.

It has now been officially stated that nuclear deterrence has, in practice, been so crude that the only option has been a massive all-out strike. In Schlesinger's words "massive preplanned strikes in which one would be dumping literally thousands of weapons" on the enemy. The highly sophisticated deterrence theories, involving bargaining, limited retaliation and the like, worked out with enormous intellectual effort by strategic analysts, have, therefore, had absolutely no effect on official nuclear policies. But bad though this situation is, the consequences of changing to a more flexible strategy of the type now being adopted are even worse. The main advantage of this policy is that, in contrast to a counterforce policy, it requires fewer rather than more nuclear weapons. The current US nuclear stockpile is from 10 to 100 times as murderous and destructive as it need be to satisfy the requirements of nuclear deterrence. "Therefore", York says, "our highest-priority objective for the immediate future should be to reduce greatly the current level of 'overkill'."

York explains that opinions about how many nuclear weapons are really needed for deterrence vary over an extremely wide range. For example, shortly after leaving the post of Special Assistant to the President (Kennedy) for National Security Affairs, McGeorge Bundy wrote: "In the real world of real political leaders—whether here or in the Soviet Union—a decision that would bring even one hydrogen bomb on one city of one's own country would be recognized in advance as a catastrophic blunder; ten bombs on ten cities would be a disaster beyond history; and a hundred bombs on a hundred cities are unthinkable."

Why is it, if one or 10, or maybe a few hundred nuclear weapons on target, are all that are needed to deter, that the USA possesses more than 25,000? And why so much total explosive power? Similarly, why has the Soviet Union deployed a comparable nuclear force?

These numbers are *not* the result of a careful calculation based on the same political, military or strategic goals, or on a rational assessment of external threats. Instead, they are purely rationalizations after the fact.

The Irrationality of Nuclear Doctrines

Any policy based on nuclear weapons must be irrational. This is particularly obvious for policies based on the use of nuclear weapons in Europe.

Soviet and American views differ on when and how tactical nuclear weapons would be used in a European war. NATO's plans for the defence of Europe, though, are based on an awesome bluff. On the one hand, NATO says that a significant attack by the Warsaw Treaty Organization (WTO), even if non-nuclear, would be countered with nuclear weapons. But this would set in motion a series of events leading to the certain destruction of most European cities, and the death of most of its people.

No sane European political leader would be willing deliberately to initiate such a chain of events. But the public admission of such unwillingness would, it is said, "undermine the credibility of the deterrent". The belief is that this would increase the probability of an attack.

Nevertheless, there doubtless are (or will be) some irrational political and military leaders who actually *would* destroy Europe in order to save it. And if such people should have their fingers on the trigger at the crucial moment, they might bring about a nuclear holocaust. In short, NATO's bluff could be called and Europe could be utterly destroyed.

Whether or not a nuclear war will take place in Europe will be determined at least as much by NATO deployments and doctrines as by those of the WTO forces. However, what will happen to Western Europe when a nuclear war takes place will be almost entirely determined by what the Soviets actually do with their nuclear weapons (and, of course, vice versa). The larger NATO weapons are mainly intended for use against targets in Eastern Europe—and such NATO weapons as may be exploded in Western Europe will, hopefully, be targeted so as to limit collateral damage as much as possible.

Take, for example, the Soviet medium-range SS-4 and SS-5 ballistic missile equipped with megaton warheads. Six hundred such missiles are deployed. These contain about 10 times as much explosive power as all other tactical types combined.

It is impossible to know just how the USSR plans to use these weapons, but it is relatively easy to say what kind of targets they would be effective against. Because of their great power, their relatively poor accuracy (a few kilometres), their peculiar range (covering all Europe, and not much more, from European URSS) and their vulnerability (they are more vulnerable than more modern types to a pre-emptive attack), they would be most effective in early strikes against governmental and major military command centres, major communications centres, large transportations centres like harbours and railyards, manufacturing facilities, and civil and military airports. These targets are mostly in or near large cities. In fact, a list of them would be, for all practical purposes, simply a list of the large cities of Western Europe, and a lot of smaller ones besides.

We can, therefore, be reasonably sure that the majority of these 600 Soviet missiles are at this moment targeted against the centres and suburbs of the cities of Western Europe. They are likely to be launched in the initial stage of a nuclear war, perhaps immediately after the "bluff" is called.

The bombardment of Western Europe by just these 600 ballistic missiles can, as Professor York has shown, easily kill virtually the entire urban population by *blast alone*. In addition, if a large portion of the warheads are exploded on or near the ground, then a major fraction of the rural population can also be killed by nuclear fallout—and so can a very large number of people outside Europe.

The use of even a fraction of NATO's nuclear weapons will, of course, obliterate Eastern Europe. In short, if there comes nuclear war in Europe, society as we know it will cease to exist. Europe will quickly be reduced to a radioactive desert.

If the use of current types of nuclear weapons in Europe is not a credible strategy, what should be done? One solution which has been suggested is to provide a range of nuclear weapons specifically designed for use in a possible European conflict situation. The military commander, it is said, should have weapons (like the so-called neutron bomb) capable of effective use for achieving his military objectives. Particularly recommended by advocates of this type of solution are low yield and very accurate nuclear weapons.

At first sight, this solution may seem attractive, particularly from the point of view of military tactics. *But there are fundamental weaknesses in any policy depending upon the use of tactical nuclear weapons.* Few would be confident that this or any other feasible policy would, in practice, prevent armed conflict involving the major powers from escalating to an all-out nuclear war so long as any nuclear weapons, regardless of type, are used. And there is no guarantee, or even likelihood, that the opponent will adopt similar tactics. In particular, the introduction of very low-yield (less than a kiloton) nuclear weapons would blur the present distinction between conventional and nuclear weapons. It is of *paramount importance* that an absolute "firebreak" should be maintained between nuclear and conventional war.

I go even further than those who believe that a war in which any nuclear weapons are used will escalate all the way to a nuclear world war in which all, or the bulk, of the nuclear weapons in the arsenals are used. I believe that *any* war in Europe would escalate in this way. In other words, any significant hostile action across the German border is, in my opinion, almost bound to escalate to a nuclear world war. To believe otherwise is to believe that one side will surrender while it still has a large arsenal left. Those that have experienced war in Europe know that countries at war do not surrender under these conditions, particularly when emotions are as high as they are in the midst of a violent war.

The only sensible policy for the nuclear weapons powers is to reduce their nuclear arsenals as a step to the total abolition of nuclear weapons.

6

New Nuclear War Fighting Weapons in Europe

MANY of the 7000 or so nuclear weapons in Western Europe were put there during the late 1950s and early 1960s. Since nuclear weapons have a lifetime of about 20 years, these are about due for replacement. In the meantime, new types of nuclear weapons have been developed and the plan is to replace the old nuclear weapons with some of these new types—a process often misleadingly called "modernization".

Among the new types of nuclear weapons planned for NATO are Pershing II missiles and ground-launched cruise missiles. These weapons are so accurate as to be perceived to be more suitable for fighting than deterring a nuclear war. Although less accurate than the American weapons, the Soviet SS-20 intermediate-range ballistic missile is accurate enough, or will soon be made so, to be regarded as a nuclear war fighting weapon, given the large explosive yield of its warhead. SS-20s are being deployed.

These new nuclear weapons increase the probability of nuclear war in Europe because they will become firmly integrated into military tactics and strategies. This will, in time, remove the barriers to the use of nuclear weapons because once a war begins the military machine operates as preplanned. The tactical plan cannot be changed in the heat of battle. This objection applies, of course, to all nuclear weapons designed for a specific front line battlefield use, such as the enhanced radiation weapon, or neutron bomb as it has come to be known. The military use of these weapons demands their early use in a war, otherwise the point of having them would be lost. There is, for example, no point in deploying nuclear weapons for use against tanks unless the weapons are used before the enemy's tanks have penetrated far into one's territory.

The SS-20

The Soviet SS-20, a two-stage mobile missile, was first deployed in 1977. About 150 were deployed in mid-1980, about 60 per cent targeted on Western Europe and the rest targeted on China. The Ural Mountains is the dividing line between the deployment areas. The missile is transported on and launched from the same land vehicle, and carries three multiple independently targetable re-entry vehicles. The missile's range with these warheads is said to be about 5000 km.

The yield of each SS-20 warhead is estimated by Western sources to be between 150 and 500 kilotons and the accuracy is said to be about 400 m. The production rate of the missiles is about 40 or 50 a year, and more than one missile may in the future be deployed for each launcher. The SS-20s are replacing the old SS-4s and SS-5s, one for one. The SS-4, of about 2000 km range, and the SS-5, of

Major Eurostrategic nuclear weapons

State	Weapon designation	Year first deployed	Max. range (km)	No. deployed in 1979
Missiles				
USSR	SS-4	1959	2000	390
	SS-5	1961	3700	80
	SS-12	1969	~800	72
	SS-20	1977	4000	~120[b]
	SS-N-5	1964[a]	~1200	18
USA	Pershing IA	1962	~750	108[c]
	Pershing IA	1962	~750	72[d]
	Pershing II	(1983)	~1600	0
	GLCM	(1983)	2500	0
UK	Polaris A-3	1967	4600	64
France	S-2	1971	3000	18
	M-20	1977	5000	64

State	Weapon designation	Year first deployed	Max. range (km)[e]	Nuclear weapons per aircraft	No. deployed in 1979
Aircraft					
USSR	Tu-16 Badger	1955	6500	2	318
	Tu-22M Backfire	1974	9000	4	50
USA	FB-111A	1969	10000	6	66
	F-111E/F	1967	4900	2	156
UK	Vulcan B2	1960	6500	2	48
France	Mirage IVA	1964	3000	1	33

[a] On board Golf-2 submarines in the Baltic.
[b] The figure is for launchers. Probably only 80 of these are targeted on Western Europe.
[c] US missiles deployed in Western Europe
[d] Deployed in FR Germany under dual US-West German command.
[e] The maximum combat *radius*, i.e. the distance an aircraft can cover in order to reach its target area, fulfil its mission and return to its base, is considerably lower—less than half the maximum range.

about 3700 km range, were first deployed in 1959 and 1961 respectively. By 1964, 590 of them were in place.

By modern standards these old missiles are extremely inaccurate.

It might on first sight be thought that to replace inaccurate and vulnerable missiles having very large warheads and obviously planned for early use in war with more accurate, less vulnerable missiles with smaller warheads is a move in the right direction. But, as we have seen, to replace nuclear weapons useful only for deterrence by weapons seen to be usable for nuclear war fighting increases the probability of a nuclear world war. Such is the mad logic of nuclear strategy.

The Pershing II Missile

The deployment of the SS-20 is used by some NATO countries as the rationalization for the production and deployment of the Pershing II missile. This missile is being developed to replace the Pershing I missile, first deployed in 1962.

Pershing II will use the same rocket components as Pershing I. But there the similarity ends. Pershing II will be provided with a formidable new guidance system called RADAG. In the terminal phase of the trajectory, when the warhead is getting close to the target, a video radar scans the target area and the image is compared with a reference image stored in the computer carried by the warhead before the missile is launched. The computer operates aerodynamic vanes which guide the warhead on to the target with accuracy unprecedented for a ballistic missile with a range of about 1700 km. The accuracy (CEP) of Pershing II is about 45 m.

Another feature of Pershing II is the manoeuvrability of its warhead. The terminal guidance system can be preprogrammed to overshoot the target and then backtrack accurately onto it. This facility enables the warhead to evade any anti-missile defence systems which may be placed around the targets.

Pershing II has double the range of Pershing I (750 km) because it has new rocket motors and uses a new highly efficient solid fuel. The missile is the only NATO ballistic missile able to penetrate a significant distance into the USSR—it could, for example, reach Moscow from the Federal Republic of Germany. And it could cover this distance in less than 10 minutes, so that there would be virtually no warning against a surprise attack.

These very accurate missiles with penetrating capabilities threaten enemy missiles in their hardened silos, as well as other underground structures, airfield runways, and so on. Pershing IIs are, therefore, counterforce or nuclear war fighting weapons.

In December 1979 NATO decided to deploy 108 Pershing IIs, beginning in 1983, to replace the same number of Pershing Is now deployed in Europe. In addition, 72 Pershing Is are deployed in the Federal Republic of Germany under joint US–West German command.

The Ground-launched Cruise Missile (GLCM)

NATO also decided to deploy in Europe 464 GLCMs. The cruise missile is an important weapon because of the possibility of its proliferation to many countries.

Cruise missiles are not new—in fact, the German V-1 or "buzz-bomb" of World War II was a cruise missile. Soon after the war, the Americans and the Russians began developing these missiles. A variety of types were produced—surface-to-surface, surface-to-air, and air-to-surface—for tactical (short-range) and strategic (long-range) use.

In 1962 the USSR deployed the SS-N-3 Shaddock—a 450-km range cruise missile carrying a nuclear warhead—and some short-range types (mainly naval air-to-surface missiles). Current Soviet cruise missiles include the 60-km range SS-N-7, the 750-km range SS-N-12 surface-to-surface naval missile, and the 550-km range AS-6 air-to-surface missile.

In 1972 the US interest in cruise missiles revived as a "bargaining chip" to persuade the Russians to make concessions at the SALT negotiations. A number of technological advances favoured cruise missile development. The most important by far was the combination of the miniaturization of computers.

Perhaps the most important characteristic of these cruise missiles is that the ratio of the payload carried to the physical weight of the missiles is relatively very high (typically about 15 per cent compared with a fraction of 1 per cent for a typical ballistic missile).

A large number of long-range interceptor aircraft would also be required to operate with AWACS to intercept and destroy the incoming missiles, which would also be extremely costly. The deployment of cruise missiles will, therefore, escalate the arms race. A defensive system against cruise missiles is generally more expensive than the cruise missiles themselves.

The missile weighs, when full of fuel, about 1400 kg, and carries a light-weight 200-kiloton nuclear warhead. The weapon has been tested at ranges of over 3000 km but the GLCMs planned for Europe will probably have a range of about 2500 km.

Apart from their high accuracy and relative invulnerability, cruise missiles are quite cheap. In a production run of, say, 2000 missiles, the unit cost (including development costs) is likely to be less than $1 million (much less than the cost of a modern main battle tank).

Cruise Missile Proliferation

Cruise missiles have considerable potential as strategic nuclear delivery systems for smaller countries. France, for example, is showing great interest in these missiles as a potential cheap replacement for its strategic nuclear weapons as these become obsolete in the 1990s. Britain may also develop its own cruise missiles. Most industrialized countries (and possibly some Third World ones) are technically capable of producing cruise missiles indigenously. But what is often lacking is a precise knowledge of the coordinates of potential targets and accurate information about the flight path to navigate to their coordinates with the full effectiveness of the missile's guidance system. For the highest accuracy, satellite photographs are needed. This partly explains why France is acquiring military satellite capability.

Cruise missiles are so accurate that they would be formidable weapons even if equipped with conventional warheads. Their relative cheapness will make some countries seriously consider them as conventional weapons. But it would be virtually impossible to verify that cruise missiles are carrying non-nuclear rather than nuclear warheads without actually inspecting the weapons. This could complicate greatly the negotiation of future arms control treaties.

If cruise missiles do proliferate widely, they may turn out to be the most far-reaching military technological development ever. And there is little doubt that improved versions of cruise missiles will, in future, be developed in rapid succession.

Conclusions

The nuclear doctrines of both alliances, relying as they do on the use of nuclear weapons, are irrational. They are based on a bluff, and an incredible one at that. It is, therefore, foolish to expect to be given rational reasons for the deployment of new types of nuclear weapons in Europe. And, in fact, none have been given. Attempts are made to justify the new weapons as reactions to the deployment of weapons by the other side, to avoid upsetting a supposed "balance". But given the enormous number—some 12,000—of nuclear weapons already in Europe, the new ones cannot serve any reasonable military or strategic need.

Another reason for demands for the deployment of the new weapons is that some European politicians need to demonstrate for internal political purposes that they are not soft on defence issues. Other politicians seem to tend naturally towards new and more powerful weapons even though there is no good reason for having them.

It is sometimes said that the new nuclear weapons are needed to prevent certain NATO countries from feeling inferior to the Soviet Union and, therefore, becoming susceptible to pressure or even blackmail from the Soviets. This argument is a strange one. The East–West military balance is an almost impossible thing to measure in any meaningful way. The figures can be used to support almost any point of view. Some of the factors in the balance, such as morale, efficiency of mobilization, dependability of allies, and so on, simply cannot be quantified.

There is little doubt that the West is much superior in most areas of military technology, although the gap between the East and West is closing. And it certainly cannot be shown that the West is generally militarily inferior to the East.

One reason why it is said that NATO is inferior and threatened by the Warsaw Treaty Organization is to justify arguments in NATO countries for increased military spending (and no doubt the same arguments are used for this purpose on the other side). The groups that argue in this way usually include in their arguments the demand for new types of nuclear weapons.

The real reason why new types of nuclear weapons are being, or will be, deployed in Europe is that military technology has made them available. And once available, politicians cannot resist the very strong political pressures that build up for their deployment.

Given the current drift to nuclear war, we should be moving towards nuclear disarmament rather than deploying weapons that will be seen to be suitable for fighting a nuclear war. Both sides should show restraint in their nuclear deployments and negotiate significant reductions in their nuclear arsenals.

It is particularly important that this should happen in Europe. It is, after all, in Central Europe that the opposing armies stand face to face. And it is Europe that is most likely to be utterly destroyed first in a nuclear war. Europeans, therefore, have excellent reasons for resisting irrational but extremely dangerous new weapon deployments.

7

The Effects of Nuclear War

ONLY about one in four people in the world is old enough to remember the atomic bombings of Hiroshima and Nagasaki, 35 years ago. But as our memory of the awesome damage done and the terrible suffering caused by the atomic bombs (euphemistically called "Little Boy" and "Fat Man") grows dim, the probability of a nuclear world war increases.

The nuclear weapons in today's arsenals have a total explosive power equivalent to that of more than a million Hiroshima bombs. There are nuclear weapons in the arsenals each a thousand times more powerful than the bomb which destroyed Hiroshima. Such a weapon has an explosive power greater than that of all the explosives used in all the wars in history.

The consequences of a nuclear war are unimaginable. But a hint, although only a hint, is given by the former inhabitants of Hiroshima and Nagasaki.

"Friends, Please Forgive Us"

Kataoka Osamu, a teenage schoolboy at the time, was in Hiroshima when the atomic bomb exploded. His account of the disaster is far more eloquent than any scientific description can be.

> I looked out of the window at the branch of a willow tree. Just at the moment I turned my eyes back into the old and dark classroom, there was a flash. It was indescribable. It was as if a monstrous piece of celluloid had flared up all at once. Even as my eyes were being pierced by the sharp vermilion

flash, the school building was already crumbling. I felt plaster and roof tiles and lumber come crashing down on my head, shoulders, and back. The dusty smell of the plaster and other strange smells mixed up with it penetrated my nostrils.

I wonder how much time passed. It had gradually become harder and harder for me to breathe. The smell had become intense. It was the smell that made it so hard to breathe.

I was trapped under the wreckage of the school building. . . . I finally managed to get out from under the wreckage and stepped out into the schoolyard. It was just as dark outside as it had been under the wreckage and the sharp odor was everywhere. I took my handkerchief, wet it, and covered my mouth with it.

Four of my classmates came crawling out from beneath the wreckage just as I had done. In a daze we gathered around the willow tree, which was now leaning over. Then we began singing the school song. Our voices were low and raspy, with a tone of deep sadness. But our singing was drowned out by the roar of the swirling smoke and dust and the sound of the crumbling buildings.

We went to the swimming pool, helping a classmate whose leg had been injured and who had lost his eyesight. You cannot imagine what I saw there. One of our classmates had fallen into the pool; he was already dead, his entire body burned and tattered. Another was trying to extinguish the flames rising from his friend's clothes with the blood which spurted out of his own wounds. Some jumped into the swimming pool to extinguish their burning clothes, only to drown because their terribly burned limbs had become useless. There were others with burns all over their bodies whose faces were swollen to two or three times their normal size so they were no longer recognizable. I cannot forget the sight of those who could not move at all, who simply looked up at the sky, saying over and over, "Damn you! Damn you!".

Our gym teacher had come to the swimming pool too. Though he was moving about energetically, the sight of his burned and swollen body and his tattered clothes made everyone's heart sink. We all began to cry. But he gave us directions and encouraged us in a firm voice, urging us to gather together our friends who had lost their sight or were badly injured and to leave the burning school building behind.

There were others who could not move at all and there were probably many who were still trapped beneath the burning wreckage of the school. Were we to run away and leave them behind without caring at all? No. . . . But there was nothing we could do, nothing. Friends, please forgive us.

"Little Boy" and "Fat Man"

8:15 am—atomic bomb released—43 seconds later, a flash—shock wave, craft careens—huge atomic cloud
9:00 am—cloud in sight—altitude more than 12,000 meters

So says part of the flight diary of "Enola Gay", the B–29 which dropped the atomic bomb which obliterated Hiroshima on 6 August 1945.

The bomb, which exploded 600 m above the centre of the city, had the explosive power of 12,000 tons of TNT. This enormous explosion—five thousand times more powerful than that produced by any previous bomb—was obtained by the fission a mere 700 g of uranium–235, out of the 60 kg or so of uranium–235 in the bomb. Such is the efficiency of even a most primitive nuclear weapon.

"Little Boy" was a crude device—nearly 3 m long and weighing 4000 kg. A modern designer could produce a nuclear weapon having a yield of a hundred kilotons and more with, say, 20 kg of uranium–235. And if he used it to trigger a hydrogen bomb, he could produce an explosion a thousand times more powerful.

The atomic bomb used to destroy Nagasaki exploded 500 m above the city at 11:02 am on 9 August 1945. It is thought to have had a yield of some 22,000 tons. Plutonium–239 was the fissile material used in this bomb. About 1.3 kg were fissioned out of some 20 kg in the bomb. "Fat Man" was about 3 m long, 1.5 m wide, and weighed 4500 kg. Today's nuclear warheads are small and streamlined. Some 8-in nuclear artillery shells, for example, have about the same yield as the first atomic bombs. And a Minuteman III ICBM warhead has an explosive power of about 350 kilotons and a weight of about 150 kg.

The staggering advances made in nuclear warhead design indicate just how unrestrained the qualitative arms race between the United States and the USSR has been since World War II.

The Number Killed

Hiroshima is built on a plateau: the city was damaged symmetrically in all directions. The damage to Nagasaki, built on mountainous ground, varied considerably according to direction. But the death rate at given distances from the hypocentre (the point on the ground directly below the centre of the explosion) was about the same in both cities.

Almost all of those within 500 m of the hypocentres when the bombs exploded died by the end of 1945. About 60 per cent of those within 2 km died: about three-quarters of them in the first 24 hours.

The number of people in Hiroshima at the time of the bomb is not very well known. Tens of thousands of troops and Korean forced labourers were there, for example. But the exact number is very uncertain. The best estimate is that about 350,000 were in the city.

By the end of 1945, 140,000 of these people had died. Even this large figure may be an underestimate. Many thousands of people were reported missing in the 1950 National Census. The number that initially survived but died in the next few years is unknown. And so is the fate of the 37,000 or so people who came into Hiroshima within the first week of the bombing.

About 280,000 people are thought to have been in Nagasaki when the bomb exploded. According to the best estimate, some 74,000 died by the end of 1945. There were many Koreans in Nagasaki too. The exact number of them killed by the bomb is not known. The number of Nagasaki A-bomb victims who died after the end of 1945 may never be known.

The number of people killed by "Little Boy" and "Fat Man" probably greatly exceeds a quarter of a million, a staggeringly high death rate of over 40 per cent.

Blast

Those killed immediately were mainly either crushed or burned to death. The combined effect of thermal radiation and blast was particularly lethal. Many of those burned to death in collapsed buildings would have escaped with only injuries had there been no fires. But as it happened, an area of 13 km^2 in Hiroshima and 7 km^2 in Nagasaki was reduced to rubble by blast and then to ashes by fire. The difference in area was due mainly to the different terrain.

About one-half of the energy generated by the atomic bombs was given off as blast. The front of the blast moved as a shock wave—a wall of high-pressure air, spreading outward at a speed equal to or greater than that of sound. It travelled about 11 km in 30 seconds.

The shock wave was followed by a hurricane force wind. But as the shock wave travelled outward, the pressure behind it fell below atmospheric pressure and eventually the air flowed in the inward direction. Thus, a supersonic shock wave was followed by an exceedingly powerful wind and then, after a deathly instant of stillness, a violent wind blew in the opposite direction.

At Hiroshima all buildings within 2 km from the hypocentre were damaged beyond repair by a blast of up to 3 tons per square metre. Casualties due to blast were particularly severe within about 1.3 km of the hypocentre; this blast reached a pressure of 7 tons per square metre.

Fire

About one-third of the total energy generated by the bombs was given off as heat. The fireballs produced by the nuclear explosions instantly reached temperatures of the same magnitude as that of the Sun (several million degrees Centrigrade). The fireballs grew to their maximum diameters of about 300 m within a second, when the surface temperatures were about 5000°C.

At a distance of 500 m from the hypocentre in Hiroshima nearly 60 cal/cm^2 of thermal radiation were emitted in the first 3 seconds—a heat 900 times as searing as the Sun. Even at a distance of 3 km from the hypocentre, the heat in the first 3 seconds was about 40 times more than that from the Sun. The heat at Nagasaki was even more intense; twice as much as that at Hiroshima.

The heat was sufficient to burn exposed human skin at distances as great as 4 km from the hypocentres. Many people caught in the open within about 1.2 km from the hypocentres were burned to death; a lot were simply vaporized.

Violent firestorms raged in Hiroshima and Nagasaki. The one in Hiroshima was particularly severe, lasting for half a day. It completely consumed every combustible object within 2 km from the hypocentre.

Moisture condensed around rising hot ash particles as they came into contact with cold air. Heavy rain consequently fell on the two cities. But not clean rain. The odious liquid which fell was highly radioactive and oily, known to this day as "black rain".

Hiroshima had about 76,000 buildings before the bomb was dropped. Two-thirds were destroyed by fire; about a quarter of Nagasaki's 51,000 buildings were totally destroyed, and many more seriously damaged. In the midst of such extensive damage, effective fire-fighting was impossible. In any case, there was no water.

Ionizing Radiation

About 15 per cent of the energy generated by the bombs was given off as ionizing radiation. About a third of this was emitted within 1 minute of the explosion. This is called initial radiation. The remainder, called residual radiation, was emitted as radioactivity.

The initial radiation dose at the hypocentre in Hiroshima was about 24,000 rads. In Nagasaki the dose at this distance was probably about 29,000 rads.

One-half of a large number of people receiving a whole-body radiation dose of 400 rads (air dose) will die. Virtually all of those exposed to whole-body radiation of 700 rads or more will die quickly. Exposed people within about a kilometre of the Hiroshima and Nagasaki bombs are thought to have received doses of about 400 rads.

Those exposed to large doses of radiation generally rapidly became incapacitated, and suffered from nausea and vomiting, the first symptoms of radiation sickness. They later typically vomited blood, developed a high fever, had severe diarrhoea and much bleeding from the bowels. They usually died unpleasantly within about 10 days.

Smaller doses of radiation produced a wide variety of symptoms, including nausea, vomiting, diarrhoea, bleeding from the bowels, gums, nose and genitals.

There was often a total loss of hair, fever, and a feeling of great weakness. Resistance to infection was markedly decreased. Septicemia was a frequent cause of death.

Late Effects

Most of the survivors still alive at the end of 1945 appeared to be reasonably healthy. But later a variety of illnesses—including eye diseases, blood disorders, malignant tumours and psycho-neurological disturbances—began to appear.

The delayed effects are the really unique, and perhaps the most terrifying, consequences of the atomic bombs.

Leukemia among survivors increased fast for about a decade, when the mortality rate reached a level about 30 times higher than that of non-exposed Japanese. Thirty-five years later, it still has not fallen to the national average.

The incidence of other malignant tumours—thyroid, breast, lung, salivary gland, bone, prostate and so on—has been, and still is, higher among survivors than among the non-exposed.

Children born to women pregnant when the bombs exploded show an increase in some congenital malformation, particularly microcephaly (abnormally small size of the head), resulting in mental retardation.

From experiments with animals and other evidence, genetic damage is undoubtedly caused by radiation. But, surprisingly, there is an apparent absence of genetic damage in survivors exposed to radiation from the atomic bombs.

A number of reasons have been suggested by experts for this absence. Among them are:

- the number of survivors involved, and the radiation doses received by them, are such that too few of the children examined showed genetic effects (even though these may have been present) to be statistically significant;
- the research methods used to search for effects are insufficiently sensitive;
- the mutations induced will show up only in second, or even later, generations;
- there may have been a large number of spontaneous abortions.

The absence of observed genetic abnormalities certainly does not mean that radiation does not produce genetic damage.

Social and Psychological Effects

The social and psychological effects of the atomic bombings were extremely severe. The communities disintegrated. The social services collapsed. Many people went mad or committed suicide. Thousands of children became orphans.

There is still today a disproportionate number of aged among the survivors. Fear of malformed offspring often prevents marriages, and unusual susceptibility to disease and fatigue often threatens employment.

The ratio of sick or injured among the survivors is almost twice the national average.

But perhaps the most tragic after-effect of those first atomic bombings is the fear in young offspring of the survivors that they may get some dread disease, like cancer, because, not they, but their parents, were exposed to radiation. These young people also fear that they may breed deformed babies because of the experience of their parents, or even grandparents. This effect on the innocent must surely be one of the most wicked consequences of nuclear weapons.

Clinical descriptions of the medical effects of radiation cannot convey the magnitude of them as well as the words of someone who has experienced them. One such person was Futaba Kitayama, then a 33-year-old housewife, who was 1.7 km from the hypocentre of the Hiroshima bomb. She has described her experiences in a Japanese journal:

> Someone shouted, "A parachute is coming down!" I responded by turning in the direction she pointed. Just at that moment, the sky I was facing flashed. I do not know how to describe that light. I wondered if a fire had been set in my eyes.
>
> I don't remember which came first—the flash of light or the sound of an explosion that roared down to my belly. Anyhow, the next moment I was knocked down flat to the ground. Immediately, things started falling down around my head and shoulders. I couldn't see anything; it seemed pitch dark. I managed to crawl out of the debris.
>
> Soon I noticed that the air smelled terrible. Then I was shocked by the feeling that the skin of my face had come off. Then, the hands and arms, too. Starting from the elbow to the fingertips, all the skin of my right hand came off and hung down grotesquely. The skin of my left hand, all five fingers, also came off.
>
> What happened to the sky that had been such a clear blue one only a moment ago? It was now dark, like dusk. I ran like mad toward the bridge, jumping over the piles of debris.
>
> What I saw under the bridge was shocking: Hundreds of people were squirming in the stream. I couldn't tell if they were men or women. They looked all alike. Their faces were swollen and gray, their hair was standing up. Holding their hands high, groaning, people were rushing to the river. I felt the same urge because the pain was all over the body which had been exposed to a heat ray strong enough to burn my pants to pieces. I was about to jump into the river only to remember that I could not swim.

I went back up to the bridge. There school girls, like sleepwalkers, were wandering about in confusion.

When crossing the bridge, which I did not then recognise, I found all its parapets of solid ferro-concrete had gone. The bridge looked terribly unsafe. Under the bridge were floating, like dead dogs or cats, many corpses, barely covered by tattered clothes. In the shallow water near the bank, a woman was lying face upward, her breasts torn away and blood spurting. A horrifying scene. How in the world could such a cruel thing happen? I wondered if the Hell that my grandmother had told me so much about in my childhood had fallen upon the Earth.

I found myself squatting on the centre of the parade ground. It must not have taken me more than two hours to get to the parade ground. The darkness of the sky lessened somewhat. Still, the Sun, as if covered with a heavy cloud, was dim and gloomy.

My burns started paining me. It was a kind of pain different from an ordinary burn which might be unbearable. Mine was a dull pain that was coming from somewhere far apart from my body. A yellow secretion oozed from my hands. I imagined that my face also must be in this dreadful shape. By my side, many junior high school students were squirming in agony.

They were crying insanely, "Mother! Mother!" They were so severely burned and blood-stained that one could scarcely dare to look at them. I could do nothing for them but watch them die one by one, seeking their mothers in vain.

As far as I could see with my declining eyesight was all in flames.

Steadily, my face became stiffer. I put my hands carefully on my cheeks and felt my face. It seemed to have swollen to twice its size. Now I could see less and less. Soon I would not be able to see at all. I kept walking. I saw on the street many victims being carried away by stretcher. Carts and trucks, heavily loaded with corpses and wounded who looked like beasts, came and passed me. On both sides of the street, many people were wandering about like sleepwalkers.

Types of Nuclear Weapons

A-bombs

The basic nuclear weapon is the fission bomb, or A-bomb as it is often called. A fission chain reaction is used to produce a large amount of energy within a very short time—roughly a millionth of a second.

The fission occurs in a heavy material such as uranium or plutonium. Neutrons are used to cause nuclei of atoms of the material to break up (or fission). Two materials are of interest—uranium–235 and plutonium–239. When a fission occurs in these materials a large amount of energy is released, the original nucleus is split into two radioactive nuclei, and several neutrons are released. These neutrons can be used to produce a self-sustaining chain reaction. A chain reaction will take place if at least one of the neutrons released in each fission is used to produce the fission of another heavy nucleus.

There exists a critical mass of uranium or plutonium—the smallest amount of the material in which a self-sustained chain reaction will take place. The critical mass depends on the nuclear properties of the material used for fission, the density of the material (the higher the density the shorter the average distance travelled by a neutron before causing another fission and therefore the smaller the critical mass), the purity of the material (if other materials are present some neutrons may react with their nuclei instead of causing fission), and the physical surrounding of the material (if, for example, the material is surrounded by a medium which reflects neutrons back into the material, some of the neutrons may be used for fission which would otherwise have been lost, thus reducing the critical mass).

In a nuclear explosion exceedingly high temperatures and exceedingly high pressures build up in an extremely short time (one-half of a millionth of a second or so corresponding to the time taken for about 55 generations of fission). The mass of fissile material begins, therefore, to expand at very fast speeds (initially about 1000 km/sec. In less than a millionth of a second, the size and density of the mass of fissile material becomes sub-critical and the chain reaction stops. The designer of the explosive device aims at keeping the fissile material together, against its tendency to fly apart, long enough to get sufficient fissions to produce an explosive power (called the yield) reasonable for his purpose.

H-bombs

The maximum explosive yield achievable by fission weapons is limited because the chain reaction can in practice only be sustained for a relatively short time. But nuclear weapons which derive energy from the fusion process can be made to have extremely large explosive yields. There is no critical mass for the fusion process and, therefore, in principle there is no limit to the explosive yield of fusion weapons, or H-bombs as they are often called.

The fusion process is the opposite of that of fission—heavier nuclei are formed from lighter ones. In an H-bomb the heavier isotopes of hydrogen—deuterium and tritium—are fused together to form helium. The reaction produces energy and is accompanied by the emission of neutrons.

Fission is relatively easy to start—one neutron will initiate a chain reaction in a critical mass of fissionable material. But fusion is possible only if the component nuclei are given a high enough energy to overcome the repulsive electric force between them due to their like positive charges. In the H-bomb this energy is provided by raising the temperature of the fusion material. Hence H-bombs are also called thermonuclear weapons.

In order to make the deuterium–tritium fusion reaction work, a temperature of a hundred million degrees Centigrade or so is required. This can be provided only by an A-bomb in which such a temperature is achieved at the moment of the explosion. An H-bomb, therefore, consists of a fission stage, which is an A-bomb which acts as a trigger, and a fusion stage, in which hydrogen is ignited by the heat produced by the trigger.

H-bombs are much more difficult to design than A-bombs. The problem is to prevent the A-bomb trigger from blowing the whole weapon apart before enough fusion material has been ignited to give the required explosive yield. Sufficient energy has to be delivered to the fusion material to start the thermonuclear reaction in a time much shorter than the time it takes for the explosion to occur. This requires that the energy is delivered with a speed approaching the speed of light.

In this way very large explosive yields are obtained. For example, the Soviet Union exploded an H-bomb in 1962 with a yield equal to that of 58 million tons of TNT (megatons), equivalent to about 3000 Nagasaki bombs. Even higher yields could be obtained. Such huge bombs, however, make little sense. The largest city would be completely devastated by an H-bomb of 10 megatons or so.

There is a wide variety of nuclear weapons in the arsenals. The explosive yields of American strategic nuclear weapons vary from the 40-kiloton warhead on the Poseidon submarine-launched ballistic missile to the 10-megaton warhead on the Titan II intercontinental ballistic missile. Some nuclear bombs for B-52 strategic bombers may have very high yields, perhaps much greater than 10 megatons. Soviet strategic missile warheads vary in yield from 200 kilotons to about 20 megatons. The former are carried on various submarine-launched and intercontinental ballistic missiles; the latter are on the SS-9 intercontinental ballistic missile. The Soviets may also have very high-yield nuclear bombs for strategic aircraft.

Some tactical nuclear weapons have very low yields. For example, one type of US 8-inch artillery shell has a yield of about 100 tons.

Neutron bomb

Attention has been drawn to low yield nuclear weapons by the debate on the neutron bomb. This weapon, officially called an enhanced radiation weapon, has a low yield, of about a kiloton or so, and is designed to maximize the radiation effects of neutrons while minimizing blast and heat effects. The idea is to kill the crews of tanks by radiation without causing much physical damage. Theoretically, about 80 per cent of the energy of the explosion would be carried away by neutrons and only 20 per cent by blast and heat. In practice, some neutrons would be absorbed by, for example, the material in the fission trigger needed for the fusion reaction. Nevertheless, the dominant effect of a neutron bomb would be the irradiation of living things by neutrons.

The Effects of a Nuclear War

Because nuclear weapons have so many yields, sizes and designs the proportion of the energy given off as blast, heat, and radiation would differ considerably. The energy distribution would also depend on where the nuclear weapon was exploded—under water, on the surface of the earth, or in the atmosphere. For example, an explosion on or near the ground would produce much radioactivity so that the radiation effect would be enhanced.

Roughly a half of the energy given off by a nuclear weapon would be blast, about a third heat, and the remainder ionizing radiation. Blast would cause the greatest number of immediate casualties and the greatest physical damage if the nuclear weapon were exploded over a population centre.

At the instant of a nuclear explosion the temperature of the weapon would rise to tens of millions of degrees and the pressure would rise to millions of atmospheres. At these extraordinarily high temperatures a great deal of soft X-rays would be emitted. But almost all of these would be absorbed by the air within a distance of a metre. Because the air would be at a lower temperature it would re-emit radiation at longer wavelengths so that more and more ultraviolet, visible, and infrared radiation would be produced. This would create a glowing mass of air, called a fireball. As the fireball grew, its temperature would fall so that it would remain visible for about a minute. The diameter of the fireball would vary with the explosive power of the weapon. A 20-kiloton warhead would produce a fireball about 360 m in diameter. A 1-megaton warhead would produce a fireball nearly 2 km across.

If the fireball touched the ground, much radioactivity would be produced and sucked up by the fireball. This material and the radioactive debris of the bomb would produce the radioactive fall-out. The radioactive particles would be carried along by the wind and later deposited on the ground, at distances depending on the size of the particles and the strength of the wind. If the weapon was exploded so high that the fireball does not reach the ground, there would be much less, but always some, fall-out.

A 20-kiloton bomb exploded below about 200 m would produce significant fall-out. For a 10-megaton bomb this height would be over 2 km.

The thermal radiation from the fireball could cause fatal burns and fires over a big area, depending mainly on the yield of the weapon. About a half of the people caught in the open air within about 2.5 km of a 20-kiloton nuclear explosion would be burnt to death. For a 10-megaton bomb this distance would be 20 km. For an explosion on the ground the crater produced by a 20-kiloton warhead in dry soil or soft rock would be about 100 m across. For a 10-megaton bomb the crater would be about 800 m across

Most deaths by blast would be caused by collapsing buildings or flying debris. These could occur at large distances. For example, about a half of the people within a distance of about 2 km of a 20-kiloton nuclear explosion would be killed by blast. For a 10-megaton explosion the distance would be as much as 15 km.

The effects of radiation from nuclear weapons are very uncertain, and may vary considerably according to the type of weapon and the environment and circumstances in which it was exploded. As a rough guide it can be said that about a half of the people in the open air within a distance of about 1.5 km from a 20-kiloton A-bomb, exploded more than 100 m above the ground, would die from the effects of the initial radiation. For a 10-megaton weapon the distance would be about 4 km.

The radiation from fall-out is potentially more lethal; the area downwind of a 10-megaton nuclear explosion in which a half of the people exposed in the open air to fall-out would die from radiation effects would be about 18,000 km^2. This is roughly 300 times larger than the equivalent area for prompt radiation.

We have stated earlier that if *any* nuclear weapons were used in a war the likelihood is that all, or the vast majority, of the nuclear weapons in the world's arsenals would be used. It is, therefore, pointless, and even misleading, to talk about the effects of lesser nuclear war. But clearly even a limited nuclear war would be traumatic for the region in which it occurred.

In Western Europe, for example, there are only 145 cities with populations of over 200,000. The destruction of these cities would kill over a third of the population of Western Europe.

In a nuclear world war, not only will the bulk of the urban population in the Northern Hemisphere be killed, but most of the rural population would be killed by radiation from fall-out. Many millions in the Southern Hemisphere would also be killed by radiation from fall-out.

A nuclear world war will have long-term consequences. The lethal effects of possible changes in the global climate, of a possible reduction in the ozone layer that protects us from excessive ultra-violet radiation, or of the genetic damage caused by radiation are not known. Nor are the political and economic consequences for the Southern Hemisphere of the total destruction of the economies of the Northern Hemisphere. Nor are the social and psychological consequences on survivors of the destruction of all social, medical, and technical services, of severe reductions in food supplies, of the contamination of water, and so on. They could, however, be far more severe than the direct effects of blast, heat, and radiation. No one knows whether or not human life would, in the long term, survive a nuclear war in which the existing 60,000 or so nuclear warheads were detonated.

To bring home the potential consequences of such a war Professor Rotblat has pointed out that it

> is technically possible—although not realizable—to eradicate humanity by radiation alone. The stockpiles held at present by the superpowers are some 15,000 megatons; an analysis of the types of weapons shows that of this total about 10,000 megatons is contributed by fission. Let us assume that all this megatonnage is exploded uniformly over the land area of the globe (1.5×10^8 km^2) near the surface, so as to create the maximal conditions for fall-out. A fission bomb of 1 kt produces a gamma-ray dose rate, at 1 hour after the explosion, of 7500 rads (radiation units) per hour, on a surface area of 1 km^2. Therefore, the 10,000 Mt would give rise to a dose rate of

> 510 rads per hour, at 1 hour, over the land area of the globe. The total accumulated dose by persons in the open would be 4700 rads, which is much more than needed to cause death by the acute effects of radiation.
>
> This scenario is of course entirely imaginary, but it does show that, potentially, radiation alone, without the contribution from blast and fires which are usually associated with war activities, could destroy humanity.

We may not know in detail just how devastating a nuclear world war would be, but we do know that it would be utterly catastrophic. Nevertheless, there is a propaganda campaign in some countries to play down the effects of such a war. This is because military science has made available nuclear war fighting weapons. Politicians are unable to resist pressures for the deployment of these weapons. To justify this deployment they are moving over to nuclear war fighting strategies. We are, therefore, being told that limited nuclear war is possible and may sometimes even be militarily effective and that civil defence measures could reduce casualties to some "acceptable" level.

This may be good politics, but it is not correct. It is also very dangerous. The politicians will probably become convinced by their own arguments and start a nuclear war.

8

Prospects for Peace

THE thesis of this book is that we are drifting inexorably towards a nuclear world war, largely because of the uncontrolled Soviet–American nuclear arms race. This arms race is fuelled by military research and development. The goal must, therefore, be to control military science. In the meantime, the nuclear arsenals must be reduced in size. But nuclear disarmament should take place in a way which reflects each country's demand for security. What we need is a comprehensive programme of arms control and disarmament measures leading visibly to nuclear disarmament. The programme would include conventional disarmament, measures to strengthen the non-proliferation régime, measures to control the global arms trade, and so on. In order to maintain national, regional, and world security feeling, the programme must be truly international and balanced. But the first steps must be the ratification of the SALT II Treaty, and the negotiation of a comprehensive test ban treaty and a chemical weapon treaty.

Although the SALT II Treaty is in no way a disarmament measure, its importance cannot be overestimated. Unless the SALT process is resumed there will be no progress in other arms control negotiations. Given the speed of military technological advances, it is essential that this happens soon. Otherwise, it may be too late to get the nuclear arms race under control.

Arms control and disarmament negotiations have, in fact, for many years now been making only very slow progress. The concept of general and complete disarmament, much alive during the 1950s, is still referred to in official statements and treaties but only in lip-service to an ideal of the past. Most people have even forgotten what the initials GCD stand for. Nor has there been any nuclear disarmament, the ostensible objective of negotiations during the 1960s and 1970s, in spite of the fact that most of the nuclear weapon powers have legally committed themselves to it in a number of treaties. Quite the contrary. The nuclear arms race between the USA and the USSR has continued virtually unabated for the past 30 years.

Not only has there been little progress towards disarmament, but the world has become increasingly violent.

The Increasing Frequency of War

> Throughout history men have sought peace but suffered war; all too often deliberate decisions or miscalculations have brought violence and destruction to a world yearning for tranquillity. Tragic as the consequences of violence may have been in the past, the issue of peace and war takes on unprecedented urgency when, for the first time in history, two nations have the capacity to destroy mankind. In the nuclear age, as President Eisenhower pointed out two decades ago, "there is no longer any alternative to peace".

This quotation is from a statement entitled "The Imperative of Coexistence" made by the then US Secretary of State, Henry A. Kissinger, to the US Senate Foreign Relations Committee on 19 September 1974.

"There is no longer any alternative to peace." If President Eisenhower was anticipating an era of increasingly peaceful relations between nations, he was sorely mistaken. The past three decades have been a period of increasing conflict—some would say of growing barbarism. Most of us have become inured to violence. So much so that few people realize how many wars are being fought in the world on any given day.

Since World War II there have been at least 140 wars. On average, then, a new war begins somewhere in the world every three months. For comparison, it is of interest that an American scholar, Quincy Wright, has listed 24 wars fought between 1900 and 1941.

Modern war is a very difficult activity to define. Before 1945, wars were usually formally declared. But since then not a single war has been declared. Such diplomatic niceties would be counter-productive in, for example, guerilla strategy—and so we are dependent on the subjective judgement of experts.

According to Istvan Kende, one such expert on conflict, a war is any armed conflict in which all the following criteria occur:

(1) Fighting by regular armed forces (including military police forces, and so on) at least on one side—that is, the presence and engagement of the armed forces of the government in power.
(2) A certain degree of organization and organized fighting on both opposing sides, even if this organization extends to organized defence only.
(3) A certain continuity between the armed clashes, however sporadic.

Centrally organized guerilla forces are also regarded as making war, in so far as their activities extend over a considerable part of the country concerned.

On the basis of this definition, 140 wars can be listed for the period 1945–79. The total duration of these conflicts exceeds 380 years. The territory of 75 countries (in Europe, Asia, Africa, and Latin America) were the theatres of war, and the armed forces of 85 states were involved. Since September 1945 there was not a single day in which one or several wars were not being fought somewhere in the world. On an "average day" about 12 wars were fought. The number of people killed in them exceeds 30 million.

About 85 per cent of the wars since 1945 have been civil wars, aimed at overthrowing the ruling régime, or fought for tribal, religious, minority, or similar reasons. The other 15 per cent were traditional wars in which the armies of two countries fought each other across their borders.

Shocking though these statistics are, there is as yet no sign of any decrease in the frequency of armed conflicts. Small wonder then that man has become so used to conflict that the majority of recent armed conflicts were scantily reported—or even ignored altogether—by the mass media. How many of us could name the wars now in progress? Some will not be impressed by these figures. War is, after all, by no means the only cause from which people die prematurely. Do not countless numbers die anyway from famine? And from natural disasters? Is overpopulation not a major cause? Or poverty? Or pollution? Even if war were abolished tomorrow, some will say, only a minority of the world's population would live three score years and ten. War may be bad, but are not the other killers equally bad? Or worse perhaps?

These arguments contain an element of truth, but they miss a crucial point. In Kissinger's words, "... for the first time in history, two nations have the capacity to destroy mankind". Other potential disasters, relatively slow in maturing, could be foreseen and forestalled. But a full-scale nuclear war could, in a flash, destroy the basis of our societies, and perhaps even humankind in itself.

Some may contemplate a nuclear Armageddon with no greater horror than when imagining conditions in a world inhabited by, say, 12 billion people—the predicted population 60 years from now. With this one can agree, but also here there is a great difference: even in a highly over-populated world there can be a fight for better living conditions, whereas a nuclear war can only worsen the situation of the majority of mankind.

Surprisingly, awareness of the catastrophic destructiveness of nuclear war seems to have become buried so deep in man's consciousness that he no longer actively worries about the ever-present danger that nuclear war could, in an instant, end our lives and our society. Who would have thought, 30 years ago, when the horror of the annihilation of two Japanese cities by the only nuclear weapons then existing was fresh in people's minds, that man could possibly rest easily with thousands of weapons capable of delivering literally tens of thousands of thermonuclear warheads kept on continuous alert? Can we not really believe that these weapons, with their almost incomprehensible destructive power, will never be used? We certainly act as though we do. Will it take the emergence of many new (less "responsible") nuclear weapon powers to reactivate public concern about the danger of nuclear war? Or must this wait until a limited nuclear war shocks us into action—assuming, of course, that this limited war will not escalate into a general nuclear war, destroying us all?

Nuclear Miscalculation

President Kennedy, alarmed by the dangers inherent in vast nuclear arsenals, warned that the biggest risk of the full-scale use of these weapons of mass destruction did not arise from deliberate intention, but from "miscalculation, madness or accident". The danger of a general nuclear war—by miscalculation—between the USA and the USSR would probably be at a maximum if the two great powers became involved in a conflict which had begun as a limited nuclear war between states who had acquired their own nuclear forces (a future Middle East war, for example).

Any war may escalate into a general nuclear war—a possibility which cannot be denied. A nuclear war may also be initiated by a political leader when in an irrational mental state, a possibility of the utmost concern to disarmers, or may come about by accident. If war cannot be abolished, the advocates of nuclear disarmament argue, nuclear weapons must be abolished, because the probability that they will be used, sooner or later, is unacceptably high. Even if this probability is very low in absolute terms, it is still unacceptably high since the consequences of nuclear war would be so catastrophic.

Few are confident that if nuclear weapons were ever to be used their use could be kept limited. If the choice is between surrender and escalation, then escalation it will be. The two world wars dramatically demonstrated the extraordinary intensity of feeling aroused on both sides when casualties are high and civilian privations great. In such circumstances emotion governs men's actions—reason certainly does not.

The case for nuclear disarmament rests, therefore, on the argument that, in today's world, governments cannot be relied on to behave in such a manner as to guarantee, for the foreseeable future, the non-use of nuclear weapons. And the more nuclear weapon powers there are, the stronger this argument becomes.

As might be expected, some people deny this. They argue that governments can be relied on always to behave responsibly in a nuclear armed world. Moreover, they claim that the very possession of nuclear weapons is likely to promote such responsibility, even on the part of governments previously lacking it.

The political leaders of the present nuclear weapon powers seem to believe, not very surprisingly, that their governments will behave with due restraint. But their opposition to the proliferation of nuclear weapons implies that they doubt whether other governments will.

Nuclear Deterrence—the Rationalization of Nuclear Weapons Deployment

Ever since nuclear weapons were invented, attempts have been made to justify their possession. To this end, very elaborate theories of deterrence have been developed by strategists and other intellectuals.

Many people believe that these weapons actually prevent war. It is, of course, unprovable that nuclear weapons have ever prevented war, but many firmly believe that they did so in the late 1940s and early 1950s. Be this as it may, it is certainly no longer true—nor has it been for a long time now—that the Soviets and the Americans are prevented from fighting each other mainly because of their possession of nuclear weapons.

Deterrence theories contain many basic flaws: political leaders will always behave rationally, countries will surrender rather than use all their nuclear weapons, and so on. Nevertheless, this doctrine is so ingrained into the thinking that it has almost become an article of faith. We have, as it is called, "learned to live with the bomb".

Although this doctrine has been changed on many points, as we described, it is still used as a rationalization for the introduction of new types of weapons, "to maintain and strengthen deterrence".

In this way, there has been rationalization about large numbers of new types of intercontinental ballistic missiles, nuclear strategic submarines, intercontinental strategic bombers, and, most recently, new types of nuclear weapons for Europe.

The public has become lulled into a false sense of security by those extolling the virtual of a balance of nuclear terror as a sensible policy. But the advocates of this theory have become hoist on their own petard.

A "good" policy for one country is likely to be seen by others as "good" also for themselves. If the USA and the USSR are seen to perceive that nuclear deterrence is a workable doctrine, then other countries will probably come to believe in it too. In international politics, perceptions are more important than facts.

Neither Disarmament nor Arms Control

Since World War II, literally hundreds of international meetings have taken place mainly in an attempt to control the nuclear arms race between the USA and the USSR and then to reduce the number of nuclear weapons in the arsenals of the nuclear weapon powers. But, in spite of so much talk, virtually no progress has been made towards either of these ends. How can this be explained?

A major reason for a lack of progress towards nuclear disarmament is related to the decision taken by politicians in the early 1960s to abandon attempts at the direct negotiation of general and complete disarmament and to work instead for partial arms control measures. The idea was that, by this method, it would be possible to move towards general disarmament in small steps.

By now, twenty years later, the record to date is a dismal one. The only disarmament that has taken place in the past quarter century is the destruction of stockpiles of biological weapons by the USA and possibly also by the USSR. The former has been officially announced, the latter not yet. It was possible to ban biological weapons because the military have very little, if any, interest in them. Biological agents generally die in sunlight and the weapons can, therefore, only be used at night. They are also indiscriminate and may infect friendly civilians and one's own troops. Apart from this, not a single weapon—not even a pistol, let alone an intercontinental ballistic missile—has been destroyed as a result of an international agreement. Instead, vast numbers of weapons—conventional, nuclear and chemical—of a bewildering variety of types have been developed and deployed as fast as technological developments allow. Furthermore, the international trade in arms has increased alarmingly and even the most sophisticated weapons are now sold in large quantities by the advanced nations, often even before they enter the arsenal of the producing country.

Very little attention has so far been paid to the problem of controlling and reducing conventional armaments or the arms trade, even though the greatest proportion of world military expenditure is used to acquire these weapons. Yet these weapons encourage and add to the violence of local conflicts, and the arms trade is one way in which the great powers, as suppliers, become embroiled in regional wars involving client states.

Many apologists for the arms control approach regard the Partial Test Ban Treaty (1963) as a singular success. But it has mainly functioned as an antipollution measure and, as such, it can be regarded as the first modern international treaty to control the contamination of our environment.

No one doubts that our environment would now be considerably more contaminated with radioactive material if the USA, the USSR and the UK had continued testing nuclear weapons in the atmosphere and under water. Although France and China have not stopped conducting nuclear tests in the atmosphere, they have done so much less frequently than did the other three powers. The treaty may also have prevented India, who ratified it, to explode a nuclear device in the atmosphere.

After the treaty, the USSR and the USA continued testing nuclear weapons underground at about the same rate as they had tested nuclear weapons before 1963. The Partial Test Ban has not, therefore significantly slowed down the nuclear arms race between the USA and the USSR. By underground testing, substantial progress has been made in improving the quality of small nuclear weapons, hardening weapons against anti-ballistic missiles, developing multiple independently targetable re-entry vehicles, and so on. Nothing short of a comprehensive test ban, prohibiting all nuclear tests, can be described as a success.

There is also considerable military interest in low-yield nuclear weapon tests. It is said that these are needed from time to time to check that the nuclear weapons in the arsenal still work satisfactorily. Unless this were done, confidence in the stockpiles would, according to test advocates, be lost and the military would no longer be willing to use the weapons. In this sense, a permanent comprehensive test ban would, in the long run, be equivalent to nuclear disarmament. But, for this reason some people will fight a permanent comprehensive test ban to the death.

There is little doubt that public concern over the radioactive contamination of man's environment was the main factor which induced the UK, the USA and the USSR to agree to discontinue tests in the atmosphere, in outer space, and under water. Public opinion has been aroused by a series of dramatic nuclear events prior to 1963, such as the severe radioactive contamination of a boatload of Japanese fisherman by an American thermonuclear explosion in 1954 in the Pacific, and the Soviet atmospheric explosion at Novaya Zemlya in October 1961 of the largest nuclear device ever exploded in the world—a thermonuclear weapon with an explosive power equivalent to that of 58 million tons of TNT. The fact that the force of public opinion overcame the strong objections to a partial test ban on the part of those groups within the nuclear weapon powers with vested interests in nuclear weapon testing is an object lesson. It demonstrates that if successfully mobilized again, public opinion should compel reluctant politicians to move towards nuclear disarmament. This may be the best—if not the only —hope of achieving such disarmament.

There have been somewhat more than 1220 known nuclear explosions since 1945, an average of about one a week. More than 650 by the USA, about 425 by the USSR, almost 90 by France, just over 30 by the British, 25 by China and 1 by India. About 60 per cent of these explosions took place after the test ban was implemented.

France is not a party to the treaty. Nevertheless, since 1974, it has conducted all its nuclear tests underground. China, also not a party, continues to carry out nuclear explosions in the atmosphere, at an average rate of about one every 18 months, but she carried out no tests in 1979.

In 1979, the nuclear weapon powers are known to have made 53 nuclear explosions—the USSR made 28, the USA 15, France 9, and the UK 1. But it has been reported that a nuclear test explosion (perhaps South Africa) was set off in the atmosphere over the Indian Ocean on 22 September 1979. A comprehensive nuclear test ban treaty could put a stop to most qualitative developments in nuclear warhead design.

To be worth having, a comprehensive test ban must be permanent and multilateral, with all the parties actively participating in its verification. A treaty of three years' duration, as is now being negotiated by the USA, the USSR and the UK, would be an unsatisfactory treaty—perhaps even worse than no treaty at all. It may delay, perhaps indefinitely, the negotiation of a multilateral and permanent ban.

Hot Line

The first bilateral arms control agreement between the USA and the USSR established a direct communication link between Washington and Moscow—the "hot line"—and came into force in June 1963 after the events of the 1962 Cuban missile crisis. A second hot line agreement came into force in 1971 to improve the reliability of the link by the use of communications satellites.

The hot line, intended for the exchange of messages in times of emergency, was first used by the two great powers in the 1967 Middle East War for mutual reassurance of their desire to avoid direct confrontation.

A rapid communications link between the great powers is undoubtedly of value in clarifying the intentions of the great powers at times of severe crisis and, thus, minimizing the risk of unintended war between these powers.

Other Soviet–American bilateral agreements relate to measures for reducing the risk of outbreak of nuclear war between the two powers (1971); for preventing incidents on and over the high seas

(1973); and for preventing nuclear war (1973). The first of these agreements provides for immediate notification in the event of the following: an accidental, unauthorized incident involving the possible detonation of a nuclear weapon; the detection by missile warning systems of unidentified objects.

The most significant provision in the agreement on the prevention of nuclear war is that if, at any time, relations between the USA and the USSR appear to involve the risk of nuclear war between them, then the two powers will immediately enter into consultations with each other and make every effort to avert the risk. The fact that the USA put its forces on nuclear alert during the 1973 Middle East War raises justifiably grave doubts about the effectiveness of this agreement.

The Public Misled

The arms control efforts—multilateral and bilateral—over the past 15 years have failed to produce any nuclear disarmament or even to halt the nuclear arms race between the USA and USSR. In spite of this, the public has been seriously misled into believing that steady progress is being made in disarmament. The main reason for this mistaken belief is that political leaders habitually make euphoric statements about the value of arms control treaties. Each treaty is signed with much pomp and ceremony, and to the accompaniment of speeches full of high-sounding promises of bigger and better things to come. And the preambles and articles of the treaties usually contain far-reaching commitments to further progress which are rarely, if ever, followed up.

The political leaders are, of course, aware of the almost universal human desire for a secure and peaceful disarmed world and of the considerable political benefit to be gained from paying lip-service to this desire. But perhaps not surprisingly they, and those involved in negotiating arms control treaties, take on a "professional optimism" which apparently causes them to convince themselves that substantial progress is being made. This may be a psychological necessity for those involved but it also hampers progress towards disarmament.

The Role of Public Opinion

Many citizens believe that the individual is powerless to influence the drift towards nuclear world war or to do much about the arms race or even to affect a country's military spending. However, it is a mistake to underestimate the power of public opinion. When the responsible citizen has informed himself of the the facts, he can make an educated judgement of the issues. If enough citizens then decide that a certain course of action, like nuclear disarmament, is indicated, politicians—even very reluctant ones—are likely to respond.

One thing to be understood about matters related to armaments and disarmament is that much irrationality is involved. This makes any rational discussion of the issues impossible.

We have already seen that nuclear policies are irrational. But so, for example, is the size of most military budgets. Most people believe that the size of military budgets is normally determined by a rational assessment of external threats, and of the weapons and size of armed forces needed to counter this threat. There is, however, little evidence to support this view, at least in so far as the industrialized countries are concerned. For one thing, the proportion of GNP most industrialized countries devote to military spending does not rise and fall—even in the crudest way—to reflect the climate of international relations.

Levels of military spending seem to be determined by a decision-making process which few would regard as rational. Most of us have a psychological need to feel "secure" and demand that the government provides "security" much as it provides other social needs like health, education, and so on. And "security" is related to military strength.

In many industrialized countries a military expenditure of between say 3 and 6 per cent of GNP seems, for inexplicable reasons, to satisfy this psychological need. If much less than 3 per cent is spent, the politicians are accused of "weakening our defences". If much more than 6 per cent is spent, they are accused of "wasting money on the military". Politicians usually take the easy way out and solve the "defence" problem by simply diverting the resources to the military.

Then comes the problem of what the money should be spent on. Once again, it is often difficult to relate the types of weapons bought with needs arising from conceivable threats to the country. More often it seems to be the armed service with the most powerful political lobby which gets the biggest share of the military cake. And the most modern and sophisticated, and therefore usually the most glamorous, weapons are often bought whether or not the country can be shown to need these specific weapons.

Once again, if the public knew the facts of the situation it would probably apply pressure to the politicians to change it.

The Role of the Scientists

Scientists have a special responsibility to assist efforts made to get support for measures to slow down the nuclear arms race and of nuclear disarmament. It is after all mainly due to their activities in military research and development that we are faced with the prospect of nuclear world war. If there were no military research and development, then the arms race, at least qualitatively, would soon grind to a halt.

The best way in which the scientific community could help would be in the dissemination of knowledge about the dangers of an uncontrolled arms race and the urgent need for nuclear disarmament. It must be emphasized that most of the facts about this are uncontroversial. Nevertheless, it is not easy to mobilize scientists to take action to this end.

One problem is the sheer number of scientists working worldwide only on military research and development—about 500,000. The number of scientists actively interested in disarmament matters, on the other hand, is depressingly small. The number that have, for example, attended the Pugwash Conferences on Science and World Affairs over the 25 years or so that they have been held is about a mere 1000. And only a very small fraction of these are engaged full-time on disarmament or related studies. It is hard to avoid the conclusion that scientists are on the whole little interested in the potential social consequences of their work, even when these consequences are as disastrous as a nuclear world war.

Two things should be done to alter this state of affairs. Firstly, scientific professional bodies of physicists, engineers, chemists, and so on, should inform their members of the consequences of military science. Secondly, universities should ensure that science undergraduates are told about the consequences of the application of their branches of science and technology. The scientific community as a whole should ensure that the effects of the nuclear arms race are known to military scientists.

The Role of the Trades Unions

One barrier to disarmament is the belief that large defence industries and high levels of military spending increase employment and improve living standards. Workers often resist any suggestion that military money should be cut. This is particularly so in times of economic recession when great pressures occur to, for example, increase the sales of arms abroad. The truth is, however, quite different from the belief. It is important that trade union leaders realize this and work for the control of the arms race. Unless they do it is hard to see how there can be any disarmament.

Many economists now realize that by reducing the resources available for investment, military spending by developed countries slows down their economic growth. The reasons for this have been discussed by, for example, the American economist Seymour Melman. He maintains that the US military economy has for many years now been so large as to cause the civilian economy to decline. His theory is that a high level of military spending is a major contributor to inflation and unemployment.

According to the 1978 UN report *Economic and Social Consequences of the Arms Race and of Military Expenditures* about 60 million people, equivalent to the entire labour force in manufacturing industries in the whole of Europe, are engaged in military or military-related occupations. (About 26,300,000 of these are in the armed forces.)

Many of the people working for the military are highly qualified.

The most highly qualified are those working in research and development. The UN report suggests that military research and development absorbs scientific and technological capabilities 10 times as great as are available to all the developing countries. As we have seen, about 400,000 of the world's most highly qualified physical scientists and engineers work on military R&D; this number is about 40 per cent of the world's research scientists and engineers.

There will be severe economic and social consequences in those countries which waste much of their research effort on military research and development. The situation in the USA has recently been described by Professor Lloyd Dumas, an economist at the University of Texas. He points out that more than one-third of the "engineering and scientific personnel in the US" are employed in the development of military-oriented technology, and have been for two or three decades or more.

Dumas convincingly lays the myth of the "spin-off" from military to peaceful technology and points out the decline in the number of US innovations over the period 1953–73, compared to those of the UK, Japan, the Federal Republic of Germany and France. In this comparison, Japan and the Federal Republic of Germany do relatively well. Not coincidentally, according to Dumas. These two countries "spent, on average, about 3.3 per cent and 22 per cent respectively of government R&D expenditures on defense and space over the period 1962–72, as opposed to a US average of 76.6 per cent".

Labour productivity is the key to economic success. Dumas describes the deterioration in American productivity over the past years. From 1947 to 1965, he says, output per labour-hour in the US grew at an average annual rate of 3.3 per cent. From 1965 onwards, the rate of labour productivity averaged only 1.6 per cent a year. In recent years, US productivity has been the lowest of any major Western economy.

Increased inflation and higher unemployment are also the costs paid by European countries for high military spending and considerable military research and development efforts over the past two decades. The trade unions, in their fight to improve the conditions of their members, should, therefore, actively oppose increases in military budgets. They should also campaign for decreases in military spendings.

The Role of the Churches

The churches should obviously take a firm stand against the use and even the possession of any weapon so destructive as nuclear weapons. They should preach against policies and doctrines—whether deterrent or war-fighting—based on the use of weapons of mass destruction. But it is also important that the churches focus attention on the immoral waste of resources on military activities. In this context, they could make the connection between disarmament and development.

The 1978 UN report cited above is quite clear about this issue. It points out that the problems of industrialization and of growth in the Third World, of dealing with the population explosion, the food crisis, natural disasters, and the effects of war, of pollution, of developing new sources of energy and raw materials while preserving currently available resources, of urbanization, as well as the problems of reducing poverty, of improving standards of health, diet, education and housing, all "make claims on investment, research and other resources in direct competition with military claims". Resources used for military purposes are lost for civil ones.

We must try to help the Third World develop. This can only be done if, at the same time, we oppose the arms race. I am convinced that, more than any other institutions, the churches have the moral duty to inform their congregations about the relationship between disarmament and development.

The Role of the Mass Media

The task of getting the correct information about the arms race and the need for nuclear disarmament to a broad public and to the moulders of public opinion must be done by the mass media. At present, much of the information disseminated is incorrect or propagandistic.

It is often said that whereas the Western mass media can discuss topics related to armaments, the nuclear arms race, and disarmament relatively objectively, of they choose to do so, this cannot be done in the authoritarian societies of Eastern Europe and the Soviet Union. This is, however, not necessarily true. Now that they have achieved what for all intents and purposes is effective military parity with the West, the Soviet leaders are anxious to control the arms race, mainly because of the high economic costs of continuing it. They are, therefore, not opposed to the public being told about the dangers of the arms race and the need for nuclear disarmament.

There is a fearsome responsibility in journalists and other mass media professionals to present objective information to the public in time.

The Role of the Smaller Powers

Another source of pressure on the superpowers to persuade them to move towards nuclear disarmament is the smaller powers. In particular, the non-aligned countries, now in the majority, may be able to act successfully. If those non-aligned countries most experienced and expert in arms control and disarmament, such as India, Mexico, Sweden, and Yugoslavia, hopefully assisted by some aligned ones like Canada, The Netherlands, and Romania, took the lead and agreed on an integrated programme of arms control and disarmament measures, having far-reaching nuclear disarmament as a visible goal, and presented this as the policy of the small powers at, say, the next Special Session of the United Nations General Assembly devoted to Disarmament, this could achieve useful results.